MUSTARD SEEDS

A collection of essays

by

Harry Eden

Published by

MELROSE BOOKS

An Imprint of Melrose Press Limited
St Thomas Place, Ely
Cambridgeshire
CB7 4GG, UK
www.melrosebooks.co.uk

FIRST EDITION

Copyright © Harry Eden 2014

The Author asserts his moral right to
be identified as the author of this work

Cover designed by Andrea Nairn

ISBN 978-1-909757-33-2

Printed and bound in Great Britain by:
Bell & Bain Limited, Glasgow

MIX
Paper from
responsible sources
FSC
www.fsc.org
FSC® C007785

*To Cheryl Collins
and to my daughter, Andrea Nairn,
for all your encouragement and support*

CONTENTS

CONTENTS

Chapter 1

MOSTLY ABOUT GOD AND CREATION

'Day 4: Cader Idris! Depart 9.15am. Reach Llyn Cau (lake) 11.15am, making hot progress; 'dip' + lunch till noon raised expectations of rapid conquest – accomplished 1½ hours later by sweating, straggling, ragged column – which was later washed down the mountain in three sodden groups by 'tropical' downpour! At Dolgoed vast soil wash on E & W facing slopes; bathing pool + drinking water pipe had less resistance to the strange ways of nature than we, and had vanished.

Stone bridge slightly damaged by river 1' above bridge carrying trees etc – worst deluge in 25 years according to some reports.'

This is perhaps the most eventful report in the log book of an Oxfordshire school's outdoor pursuits centre in the south of the Snowdonia National Park. This group was part of a project which annually took the whole of one year group of 13- to 14-year-olds for five days in parties of 15 to an isolated farmhouse, which only provided the most basic necessities of living.

Further enquiries revealed that, as the boys walked down the mountain, lightning struck the ground between the three groups. The bridge mentioned was normally a good 12 feet above the level of the river. The scars of the gullies produced by this particular storm remained visible for many years afterwards...

In five days they (and for that matter the teachers) learned a great deal, not only about their particular choice of study but also about this very contrasting area of Britain, about their fellow students and about themselves. The climax of the stay was the walk up Cader Idris, the highest summit in that area. For boys that age – few of whom had done anything remotely like this before – it was a challenge; many of them surprised themselves in what they managed, or in certain cases didn't manage, to do.

The young boys began – in varying degrees – to sense the reality of the ecological relationships that were in evidence around them as they studied glacial landforms, hydrology, plant life, soil profiles, soil acidity and temperature variations within a small area: and others – less scientifically inclined – studied farming, the use of the Welsh language and the historical geography of the slate mines. While our records certainly could not meet requirements for convincing evidence, they did stimulate questions and interest in some most unlikely people and prompted some of them to go on asking questions in the same vein.

At about this time the questions raised by ecologists in the biological sciences had spread to other branches of the sciences and research work was beginning to filter from the labs to university textbooks and thence to the syllabuses of schools. The systems approach to the study of science spread to other disciplines – particularly to Geography – and students began to appreciate the relationship between rainfall, slopes, groundwater, stream flow, vegetation in any given environment and the way in which all these variables were interrelated.

One result of these experiences was that the young people became very much more aware of the power of the elements and of the interrelationship between the environment and all living matter, particularly with reference to animals and human beings. On some of the parties we used to have prayers outside in the morning before we set out, and perhaps one of the most apt was Psalm 8.

'O Lord our Governor, how excellent is thy name in all the world... When I look up at the heavens, the moon and the stars set in their place by thee, what is man that thou art mindful of him, or the Son of man that thou visitest him? For thou hast made him little lower than the angels and crowned him with glory and honour. Thou hast put all things in subjection beneath his feet and crowned him with glory and honour: all sheep and oxen and the beasts of the field, the birds of the air and the fishes of the sea.'

And as we walked along the ridge between the two summits of Cader Idris and we saw the tiny figures of other walkers far below us we really caught the sentiments of the psalmist as we saw the figures dwarfed by the mountain, and the surrounding scenery prompted the question, *'What is man that thou art mindful of him and the son of man that thou visiteth him?'* On the one hand he is so small and insignificant in the context of the three thousand foot mountain, yet on the other we had ample evidence of the effect of man upon the landscape – for the last two hundred years, at least. The clearing of the scrub oak to make way for the sheep pastures and the subsequent demise of that land use and the planting of conifers up to the thousand foot contour – not to mention the very significant scarring of the landscape by the 19th-century slate mines with their entrances to the drifts and the waste heaps near at hand – all these occurred within that time.

And this landscape illustrates perfectly the dual nature of man. Absolutely dwarfed by the mountain landscape, very much a created being – insignificant beside the greatness of the creator who brought all this into being – yet made in the image of God and therefore also a co-creator, a lieutenant, as it were, in the great scheme of creation…and delegated to share with God in creation and continuing and perfecting that which God had set in motion.

Up to this time these developments had been staged, so to speak, on a globe which – if not completely inert – was nevertheless perceived to be comparatively stable and unchanging. There had been controversial theories about continental drift, which were well supported by evidence, but at the layperson's level they seemed divorced from any real significance.

However, by the 1960s and 1970s these had been developed into the much more comprehensive science of plate tectonics – which linked continental drift to shorter term earth movements, vulcanicity and mountain building in a way which excited the imagination.

We were fortunate to have been given the printouts of seismographs from one of the West Wales coal mines, which recorded earthquake tremors – not only local ones, which might threaten the safety of the mine, but larger ones from all over the world. These ranged from relatively small tremors in Belgium and North Wales to the catastrophic events in Mexico and in Japan, which had led to significant loss of life. To be able to point out the evidence collected in South Wales about an earthquake on the other side of the world really brought home the concept of a world which was not inert but which was a dynamic and constantly changing set of interacting parts. The notion of the earth being made up of a series of plates floating – as it were – on the molten interior of the earth was challenging and exciting and really began to bring the study of rocks and fossils, oceans and mountains to life. The added discovery of the evidence which supported, for instance, the development of the Atlantic Ocean over a period of no more than 200 million years – with the varying depths of silt accumulation and of the magnetic orientation of rocks at different distances from the plate margins – all this made the study of the whole universe more exciting than ever, with its implications of a globe in which everything was totally integrated and yet dynamic.

Yet alongside these studies the young people would be studying the Biblical description of the Creation, which popular opinion perceives as being understood literally by those who follow its teachings. And unfortunately there are still Christians who believe that a literal interpretation of Biblical texts is essential for a proper understanding of God's revelation of himself.

This is an old and long running tradition, and we find instances of the problems that it can cause throughout the history of the church. It is interesting to discover that as long ago as the second century AD Origen was saying that, 'Anyone who believes that God's word can only be understood literally has a weak understanding of truth.' In the 17th century Galileo was put under house arrest for presuming to counter the official belief that the sun revolved round the earth. Also in the 17th century Archbishop Ussher of Ireland calculated – by making a mathematical analysis of dates and ages in the Bible – that the creation of the earth occurred in 4004 BC. It is possible to see in a small notebook (in Trinity College Library, Dublin) the very precise notes he made, which explain the basis of his calculations.

But perhaps the watershed between the two divergent views was established when – in 1859 – Charles Darwin published his famous essay *The Origin of Species,* and many Christians came to the conclusion that they had to opt totally and irrevocably for either a belief in the Creation or in evolution, as if they were opposing theories of the same phenomenon. The furore that this conflict created was responsible for a severe reaction in a significant section of the church in that those whose faith had not been destroyed were put so much on the defensive that only a few were able to accept the possible truth of Darwin's theories and start to readjust their interpretation of the Creation.

To understand this we have to go back to those very early times, when humans were beginning to ask questions about the world they lived in. They were certainly not as primitive as we often make them out to be, but their understanding of the natural world was quite different from ours. We shall be considering the development and understanding of the Bible in a later chapter: what we need to say now is that in the very early years of human activity in the region there were fairly widely-believed notions that the elements which dominated human existence – heat and cold, sunshine and rain, storm and earthquake, not to mention the fertility of the crops and the multiplying of herds – that all these were subject to the whims of gods who controlled them and unleashed their devastation or their riches as and when they pleased. One of the Flood stories of this early time – the epic of Gilgamesh –tells of Utnapishtim, a legendary king in the region, and relates how the gods were tired of the noise made by human beings and that they decided to destroy them by means of a great flood. However, Ea – the god of wisdom – felt sorry for Utnapishtim and told him to build a boat and take in it 'the seed of all living things'. Then the flood came, and with such fury, that even the capricious gods repented of their purpose to destroy the human race. The storm abated on the seventh day and the boat ran aground on Mount Nisir. Seven days later Utnapishtim released a dove and then a swallow and, ultimately, a raven...

Religion, therefore, was all to do with appeasing the gods – or forcing them to fall in with human requirements – and sacrifices, gifts and worship were all concentrated to that end. The stories or myths which have relayed some of these beliefs to us were simply a means of conveying these perceived truths to the community, and were later written down to ensure that the communities' beliefs survived. The origins of the Biblical beliefs derive from a group (or groups) of people who began to understand that all these agents were in fact expressions of one creator God who – far from being capricious – had one unswerving purpose, which was to create a perfect world in which the whole process was directed to one integrated and harmonious whole. So the version of the Flood story which was handed down by this culture depicted a sole creator who loved his creation and who was concerned not for himself but for those who were, like Noah, in tune with his purpose for good against evil.

Just as the ideas that are revealed to us so often start out vaguely and need to develop in understanding and articulation, so it was with the belief in one God and his Creation of the world. Early attempts to understand and to convey this new appreciation of truth were simplistic and incomplete, but true in the sense that those interpreting them had grasped the principles of creation. The principle that they had grasped was that in creation God not only began the creation of the universe but also established a set of relationships by which the process of creation could be brought to perfection. So the early chapters of Genesis describe those relationships between God, the universe – including stars and planets, land, sea and air, living matter from the simplest single cell organism to the largest plants and animals. Last of all came God's special Creation – man – made in his image and likeness, and therefore essentially a free agent, free to cooperate with God in perfecting Creation but – and this is a necessary corollary – free also to go his own way and choose whether to do good or evil, to cooperate with the creator or to strike out on his own.

By this stage you may have noticed that I have not made any attempt to prove that what I am trying to put over is true. That is because to some extent or other the great majority of people believe in God. A recent poll of religious observance in the western world recorded that the two most irreligious countries are the Netherlands and Britain, yet taking several consecutive groups of 14-year-olds of moderate academic ability from the latter country, I used to ask them to write down (confidentially) answers to questions such as:

Do you believe in God? Do you believe in the Devil? Do you believe in life after death?…and so on. To the first question the answers were always somewhere between 70 per cent and 90 per cent in the affirmative. Whether the result would have been the same had the poll been public is another matter.

Just as with the misunderstanding over the meaning of Genesis we in the 20th century have been so immersed in the scientific culture of our age that we mistakenly believe that the existence of God and the truth of the book of Genesis can be arrived at through the empirical methods of science: that we can arrive at the truth through debate and through evidence. Students of the philosophy of religion will be well versed in the classical arguments for the existence of God but, while they may move some towards a greater sympathy with the idea of faith, they can never give any idea of what faith is all about. That does not mean to say that we abandon logic in our dealings with religion but that we recognize that reason can only take us so far and no further.

The classic story that is told to illustrate this is of the great tightrope walker, Blondin. We are asked to imagine him successfully walking across the Niagara Falls, pushing a wheelbarrow. He reaches the other side and steps on to the land. He asks the nearest spectator whether he believes that he can successfully cross back to the other side. The answer is in the affirmative, whereupon Blondin invites him to get in the wheelbarrow...

Faith is what leads us to step beyond our certainties and take a risk in some course of action. It comes from within – sometimes we simply find ourselves doing something or going somewhere, motivated by an inner compunction which overrides rational hesitancy or personal distaste. What we have to realize particularly is that a great deal of faith survives in the grip of doubt. Faith which experiences no doubt is quite different. It can often mean that the person concerned has handed little over to God, and that he or she has inadvertently put themselves at the centre of the universe and –without realizing it – has usurped the place of God. There is a great difference between faith and certainty.

Let us return to our understanding of Genesis. I said earlier that the first two chapters of Genesis outline the relationship between God, man and the universe and that being human means that our relationship with God is personal. Now this term relationship is one that is constantly on our lips. Men and women talk about having a relationship. We have good or bad relationships with other people. What do we actually mean by relationship? I believe that we are saying that in a relationship we actually give something of ourselves to the other. We share; we expose; we open ourselves up to being invaded by another person. If we think of the closest relation-ship that we have – and that will probably be with a spouse or a parent – we would say that the essence of a relationship is that we are prepared to reveal ourselves to the other as we really are; the second part is that we will be prepared to put the other's needs on the same level as our own, or in other words to love them. And so it is with our relationship with God. There is a world of difference between believing that something exists and recognizing that someone is calling you to reveal and give yourself to him or her.

Now the essence of this creator God with whom we have a relationship – or, put another way –in whom we believe – is that he is the creator, and that all that he creates is good. This is underlined in the first chapter of Genesis. So God is good...and in his relationship with man he gives something of himself, some creative spirit or breath, which is directed towards the perfection of or the making good or complete that which he has created. It is as if each part of God's Creation starts off as a rough draft of the finished project. If God is allowed in (as it were) to oversee, to correct, then the development of that creation – be it a plant an animal or a human being – will gradually achieve perfection. When we establish a good relationship with someone we bring forward the process of the perfection of that person in order to enable him or her to be what God created them to be. We contribute to the successful completion of God's purpose in creation. But God also designed or had the purpose that his Creation would be one great harmonious entity, where every single part of Creation fits harmoniously into every other constituent part. In short the world (or God's whole Creation) is designed to be one completely integrated system with millions of links and variables, in which every part is able to perform its specified purpose to perfection. It is also in such a relationship, directly or indirectly, with all the other parts so that they are all mutually beneficial to the proper functioning of the whole system. It is this concept to which the Jews gave the name shalom, and the common translation – peace – is far too limited to convey what it means. Its nearest translation is harmony.

If that were the whole story then the universe would be without flaw and a perfect system. It is a state that is quite beyond our comprehension, for the fact of the matter is that in making man God was instrumental in ensuring that imperfection was introduced into the system. For, as we read in Genesis, God created man in his image and likeness and he gave him the knowledge of good and evil and the freedom to choose between them. The only way in which man could therefore assert his freedom was by choosing evil, that is by putting himself at the centre of the universe and asserting his will over other parts of the system: his ambitions, not God's. So here we have a creature with the freedom to choose his own way, not God's, and – with the same creative power – to use it for God or purely for himself. And inevitably at some point man chooses to disobey, to rebel, to sin against God and to go his own selfish – and therefore sinful – way.

More than enough has been made of the propensity of human beings for evil. Whole sections of the church and significant periods of time have emphasized the fallenness of the world and particularly of the human race. More recently we have been more aware of the damage this can cause in young people who have been told their shortcomings without ensuring that they know themselves to be of value to God and to the community. So it is very important that we take the status of being made in God's image very seriously and recognize it for the privilege and challenge that it is. The age in which we live is very actively involved in the ongoing consideration of the advances in scientific research and the attitude that humans take to it.

We need now to remind ourselves that this little word sin has been enormously misunderstood. The Greek word in the New Testament which most often translates sin is hamartia. This is a term used in archery and it means to miss the bullseye. It goes without saying that if we follow our own limited vision in our own limited strength then we are almost certain to miss the mark. And if we consistently go down that road we shall allow our judgement to be gradually warped so that we depart further and further from the path of goodness and purity. Eventually we will find humans doing the sorts of things which are so awful that the word hamartia is quite inadequate and words such as evil, devilish, pathological and depraved may still fall short of describing the awfulness of some of the acts perpetrated by human beings. We have only to scan the pages of the newspapers to realize that there are such acts committed every day of the week in one part of the world or another.

Now this situation is perceived as one of the great barriers to belief in God. Here are some classic complaints: how can a God of love allow such awful things to happen in the world? I have given up believing in God because he allowed this or that wonderful person who did so much good to be murdered, and yet Slobodan Milošević is murdering thousands of Albanians and no one can do anything about it, except create what seems to be another Vietnam War in the Balkans. My husband has worked so hard all his life and has always put me and the children first yet after just three months of retirement he has been told that he has inoperable cancer and only six months to live – how can I believe in a God of love?'

If we remind ourselves that God has created humans as free agents it follows that he has to give them the freedom to commit wicked acts and therefore there will be innocent people who will suffer. We are reminded of the text in the Bible which reads: the sins of the fathers are visited on the sons to the third and fourth generation. Of course, this prolif-eration of evil is entirely consistent with a world which is an interactive system. If every constituent part of the universe has connections with every other part then there is going to be a knock-on effect when evil deeds are perpetrated. Much more to the point we see all too clearly that things which are done with the very best of intentions – yet which turn out to have been unfortunate – at the very least can have ramifications which cause great suffering and misery. It is very easy to see how (for instance) the immigration of West Indians to Britain (encouraged by the government in order to provide low-paid labour in the transport industry) led to an underclass, the members of which have remained locked into deprivation and who have been typecast so that they have found it very difficult to be accepted as equals within the national community. Now (as a generality) that is unavoidable, but it does seem that in certain circumstances there is an interruption of that inevitability – which speaks so clearly of a God who loves his Creation – that we assume that he has altered the perceived course of cause and effect to send us a message of hope. However it is not my intention to deal with the phenomenon of miracles here, so we shall leave this till later.

In the light of all this it is not too difficult to see that the self-centredness of humans becomes compounded and you can get the sort of communal or national evil which gives rise to such horrors as the holocaust, or the terrible genocide which has been a feature of the Balkan states not just recently but for hundreds of years. We can also see how human greed can cause apparently natural disasters – such as huge landslides, which devastate whole communities – because land has been eroded by overcropping in order to feed the products of a very high birth rate. Then again we read of the devastation caused by volcanic eruptions, earthquakes and tsunamis, which from time immemorial have wreaked their havoc with invariably huge loss of life. Who is to say whether the risks of living in a volcanic area are too great or not? We tend too often to bring our own perspective to these matters and we need to realize that our obsession with living beyond our allotted four score years has a lot to do with the horror of death, rather than the assumption that a shorter life is necessarily a worse experience.

So it could be that what we may in certain instances think of as evil may simply look quite different if for instance we think of life as a gift, rather than something which is due to us as of right.

The issue can also look different if we return to the idea of creation being a process rather than an event and therefore being a graduation from the simple and crude to the more complicated and intricate. One of the perceived scourges of our modern society is the very high incidence of cancer as a killer disease. We ascribe it to a great extent as being a product of our lifestyle and are continually intimidated by the latest piece of research which suggests that our consumption of this or that is responsible for the increase in numbers of those suffering from the disease. It is also fair to say that so much has been achieved with other diseases, especially heart disease, that there are fewer diseases left which cannot be cured. Whichever explanation is relevant (if we think in terms of perfecting the world) it is not too difficult to imagine that had we – as western nations – not felt the need to spend so many billions of pounds on nuclear armament then some of the money which that demanded could have gone to advance cancer research much more quickly and its cure could have been brought forward. In much the same way we have read of some very distressing episodes which have resulted from severe earthquakes. It would be quite unfair to suggest that in some way the human misery which has resulted from these is in any way attributable to human evil. However, there promise to be much better ways of predicting the onset of earthquakes and the risk involved in building in certain areas. Added to that there are also very advanced building techniques which enable a structure to absorb shocks and ensure the safety of a building's inhabitants. In these and many other ways the threats to life and limb and the fulfilment of human life gradually become lessened as the earth moves towards maturity and ultimately perfection. In this way we can see that what would once be termed a disaster just becomes a natural hazard whose level of risk determines the priority that the community gives it.

It is very important at this juncture to outline the nature of this God of creation. He is the nucleus, the origin and the impetus behind the creation, the evolution and ultimately the perfection of the universe. God is the initiator, the first cause and the initial force which set everything in motion. But he is also the design and the purpose which produces the blueprint for its successful accomplishment. But, like the parent, he can too often almost seem like the capricious gods of the polytheists. He is angry; he is vengeful. He appears to sulk and to require payment and to hate his enemies. But, as I have mentioned earlier, these perceptions are those of faithful people whose understanding of their faith (and of the God in whom they were putting their trust) was limited. It needs constantly stressing that God is incapable of causing evil. Suffering is not sent by God; God does not wish for suffering, nor is he the agent of suffering or death. But because he has given humans free will he cannot prevent the evil that man causes by his insistence on ignoring God's law. Evil is a human trait and stems solely from man's determination to assert his independence of his creator (or father). But this poses the question – how can the perfectly natural human tendency to do without our maker develop to produce the appalling horrors of the holocaust or of the Serbian and Rwandan genocides? How does this grow into the sort of mind that produces a Harold Shipman or a Hitler? To answer this question we should return to the natural world.

One of the greatest developments of the last 30 years or so has been the science of meteorology. However, significant as that has been, it has also taught us that we still know relatively little about the mechanics of the atmosphere. What we do know, however, is that in view of the nature of fluids and the complexities of the interaction of the atmosphere and the earth we are able to see that even a very small change – be it a small bit of turbulence, a variation in temperature or a change in topography – can produce reactions immeasurably greater than the trigger which set it in motion, just as a child could develop a character whose self-regard becomes exaggerated by the irresponsible giving of the father (who is trying to assuage the guilt of never spending time with his child). More particularly, evil thrives in community. The classic novel Lord of the Flies is a telling description of the basic cruelty of young children who have yet to reach the age of real social awareness. And many people have their own experience of the things that they have done in a group which they would never have even contemplated on their own.

One of the ways in which we have endeavoured to explain this is in a belief in a personification of evil. Once more the idea comes from the Bible, which has many instances: the Devil, Beelzebub, Satan, and in one sense they are right insofar as they suggest that evil originates in human beings. But the further development of an individual person called the Devil or Satan raises more questions than it answers and it would be a better explanation to say that the name is one way of conveying that evil can be concentrated in one person and this helps to remind us that all evil is personal.

With all these things in mind I believe that we can have an adequate understanding of God without getting into the very dangerous waters of dualism – believing in two opposed gods. But God can never be omnipotent in our understanding of the word. He is in fact like the parents who know that in order that their children might grow up they have to be given the freedom to choose the way in which they go, even at the risk of going the wrong way and causing damage to themselves and to others. And sometimes, sadly, even from the worthiest of families comes a human being who somehow gets caught in the most terrible of human degradation.

But to say that God is not omnipotent, in one sense of the word, does not mean that he has no control over his Creation. There are many instances, not only recorded at the time the Bible was written but also in the succeeding centuries, where God has clearly revealed himself to humans in a very telling way. Abraham's departure from Haran and his journey to Canaan is one, the story of the Exodus and the crossing of the Red Sea another. In the New Testament we read of the birth, the death and the Resurrection of Jesus and the coming of the Holy Spirit at Pentecost; subsequently the conversion of St Paul and the gradual growth and spread of the church in its early years.

And this has happened because the power of God is one which works through a creative relationship in the whole universe, which we are gradually coming to understand. In the narrowness of our earlier understanding we have under-estimated the insistent nature of a God who fails to reveal his power and compromises his will, but who actually 'though he was in the form of God, taking the form of a servant, humbled himself.'

Chapter 2

JESUS TURNS THE WORLD UPSIDE DOWN

Christmas at St Andrews
Would never be complete
Without the children dressing up –
They always look so sweet.

This year we had an angel
Who said she'd run the show
With Alice and with Calum
And the baby all in tow.

Though rather short of shepherds
It didn't spoil the fun.
Some plays have far too many –
At least we still had one.

But then some shepherds joined her
Though she left them all behind.
Their leader wasn't bothered
And they didn't seem to mind.
It started running smoothly
Though it seemed the strangest thing.

The shepherd hadn't lost her sheep –
The kings had lost a king!

Although a king was missing
We brightly made the most
Of multitudes of pretty girls
Who formed a heavenly host.

Please will you be Joseph?
Was cried to every man.
It's not the same without him
But we'll manage if we can.

The innkeeper was confident
He bellowed every word.
With 'ROUND THE BACK' a-ringing out
His voice was clearly heard.

And where to put the instruments?
Decision quickly made.
We'll stuff them in a manger
Wherein a baby laid.

So thank you to our Mary
The shepherds and their sheep
The angels and the kings
And the person to inn-keep.

And thanks to both narrators,
The percussionist who played
And those who fixed the costumes
With needle, thread and braid.

But special thanks to Lucy
Who really did her best.
Please will you do it next year?
Will be our next request.

The above appeared in the January newsletter of a parish church and it typifies the problems that so many churches these days find and overcome – well, just – at Christmas. In it are hints of the busyness and the difficulties in a community which runs on goodwill, of finding those who are prepared to give the time to what everyone would nevertheless agree was a worthwhile – indeed an essential part – of a traditional Christmas.

Parents who would not normally come to church will come to see the Nativity and, if there is a Christingle service, it will attract a large number of people at some point prior to Christmas Day. It is easy to be cynical about the beliefs of those whose make the effort to come: nostalgia does have some element of altruism about it and the innocence of a baby and the poverty of the parents – not to mention the weakness of the whole family unit, which is pushed here or there by the requirements of those in power – all these resonate with our sensitivities towards those who feel that they too are victims of a similar tyranny.

And it would be a heart of stone that did not recognize the plight of a baby born in such circumstances and the identification with all the persecuted and weak of the world. So at this time of the year we are all willing – in the same spirit – to put our hands in our pockets and give to Crisis or The Children's Society, to those whose Christmas has been devastated by war or famine or disaster of some kind... And then comes Christmas Day, most of which is devoted to the gathering of the family, to the most significant meal of the whole year and the ritual present-giving which – at the beginning of the 21st century – is a veritable orgy of new clothing, expensive toys and gadgets, bartering, envy, disappointment and finally sheer exhaustion.

And then there is a huge gap...and those who are curious can discover that there was no celebration of the Nativity until the fourth century and in the east, at least for a time, the celebration of the Epiphany and of Christ's baptism were more important.

But in the Bible we find that the story of the Nativity is only found in Matthew and in Luke and that the earliest Gospel – St Mark – makes no reference to any incident in the life of Jesus until he appears as one of those who is baptized by John the Baptist.

Baptism was a relatively recent expression of penitence in the Jewish community and its awareness that the sad state to which God's nation had sunk since the halcyon days of David and Solomon – after successive occupation by the Assyrians, the Babylonians, the Persians, the Greeks and the Romans – and even the Jewish kings had corrupted the faith and ignored the law.

So here we meet Jesus for the first time and straight away he astonishes us by insisting on submitting himself to baptism by John. John, not surprisingly, suggests that a role reversal would be more meaningful – but Jesus insists on his own act of repentance. And by that act he is shown from the outset to be more concerned with identifying with every sort and condition of the human race. He is not so concerned at this point to identify himself with the God of Abraham, of Moses and of Elijah.

What do I mean by that? I suggest that the God who was at that time being presented to the people by the religious professionals was a God who was divisive, in the sense that society was divided up into those who were acceptable to God because of their success in keeping the law and –on the other hand – those whom God had turned away from because they had contravened his laws. But these laws – some of which might more accurately be termed misinterpretations – excluded those who had made mixed marriages with those of other religions, those whose sickness had shown that they were sinners, those who had defiled the Sabbath by doing something that the lawyers had stipulated was forbidden, those who had not observed the laws of purity – and the laws also even covered purely external signs such as special clothing and religious gestures.

At his baptism Jesus was in effect saying two things. First: whatever the benefits of the law (or indeed its essentiality) might be to society, it nevertheless divides people – it doesn't integrate them. Second: he was indirectly indicting the interpretation of the law propounded by some Jews and suggesting that in certain essential aspects it was actually contradicting the law of God; that, in certain important instances, to keep the law was to contravene God's purpose – that, for instance, everyone was obliged to go to the aid of the Samaritan, to heal on the Sabbath, to persist in constructive relationships with people who were sinners – and, since disease was the direct result of sin, it included the sick and the handicapped and particularly the lepers who were completely cut off and ostracized by society. And, of course, John protests to Jesus that it is he who ought to be receiving baptism from Jesus.

Here is an instance, the like of which seems to be repeated

frequently in the life of Jesus, where he was more concerned with building a relationship with people – more concerned with conveying his empathy with them than he was in what we might call contemporary theological truth.

Then, to set the seal on this very controversial scenario, a dove flies down and a voice is heard: this is my beloved Son; listen to him.

In modern parlance one could say that this first picture in the ministry of Jesus can be read as a sort of trailer to the main part of the film.

And now here is Jesus, who stands alongside and represents ordinary human beings, completely consumed with the sense of being inside the mind of the one who created the universe. And he forthwith leaves the company of humans and goes off into the wilderness – on retreat if you like – to listen to the God on whose behalf he is to prosecute his ministry. And we are warned at the outset that he will not be using the obvious and expected methods of winning men's allegiance.

What is the most fundamental perceived need of the whole world? Food and material goods, especially in disaster areas and in places that are severely underdeveloped. The Devil said to Jesus, 'If you are the Son of God, tell these stones to become bread.' Jesus answered, 'It is written: "Man does not live on bread alone".'

Who are the most influential, the most powerful, the most successful people? Well, first (of course) they are the politicians, the leaders of the most powerful nations, those who can command the largest armies. Jesus is led to the highest mountain and shown all the kingdoms of the world. 'All these will I give you if you will fall down and worship me,' said the Devil.

And when their stomachs are full, what do humans crave in order to satisfy themselves? Experiences – direct ones – like sex, eating, the thrills of danger, parties, drugs of all sorts – or indirect ones – such as sports, horror movies, wonders and things to marvel at.

The Devil led him to Jerusalem and had him stand on the highest point of the temple. 'If you are the Son of God,' he said, 'throw yourself down from here. For it is written: "He will command his angels concerning you to guard you carefully; they will lift you up in their hands, so that you will not strike your foot against a stone".'

So let us see just how Jesus set about his mission.

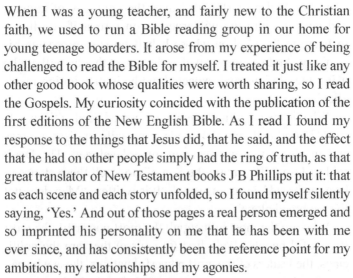

When I was a young teacher, and fairly new to the Christian faith, we used to run a Bible reading group in our home for young teenage boarders. It arose from my experience of being challenged to read the Bible for myself. I treated it just like any other good book whose qualities were worth sharing, so I read the Gospels. My curiosity coincided with the publication of the first editions of the New English Bible. As I read I found my response to the things that Jesus did, that he said, and the effect that he had on other people simply had the ring of truth, as that great translator of New Testament books J B Phillips put it: that as each scene and each story unfolded, so I found myself silently saying, 'Yes.' And out of those pages a real person emerged and so imprinted his personality on me that he has been with me ever since, and has consistently been the reference point for my ambitions, my relationships and my agonies.

And so each Wednesday night at 8 o'clock we met together and read sections of St John's Gospel and shared our reactions to Jesus as he met Nicodemus, the Samaritan woman at the well, the man who had been crippled for 38 years, the woman caught in the act of adultery and the man born blind.

One of the most vivid stories is that of the Samaritan woman at the well. Here is this historic watering place – now largely abandoned and superseded by the facilities in Sychar, half a mile away – where the disciples had just gone to procure food. It says something that these Jews were prepared not only to travel through Samaria but to stop and shop in a Samaritan town on the way. Jesus asks for water from this lone woman, who for some reason had come out of the town to draw water. Was she an outcast of some sort, as well as being a Samaritan? The conversation certainly conveys a very small proportion of what was said between them and it is clear that Jesus knows a great deal about her, almost certainly a result of her finding someone who conveyed great concern and was prepared to listen to her tale of woe. And Jesus taps in to her physical needs to take her deeper and offer her not just temporary and physical refreshment, but deep and lasting contentment and peace. And yes, she probably was rejected – for it transpires that she has had five husbands and that she and her present partner are not married. It is hardly surprising that on her return to town, having forgotten to take her water-jar (?) she wants to tell everyone to 'come and see a man who told me everything I ever did.'

Another of these encounters is told in chapter five, and concerns Jesus's healing of the man at the sheep pool. Here is a popular spa – and we can be sure that among those who came for the healing powers that it was supposed to provide there were genuine cripples such as the one in mind. But there would be many others whose illnesses were relatively slight or even imagined and many more who came as onlookers. The popular belief was that the periodic bubbling of the pool was due to an angel disturbing the water and that the first person to enter the pool at the water's disturbance would be healed. And Jesus is looking on at the scene, and the majority of the eyes would be focused on the edge of the water to see who would get in first – and those who were fittest and strongest would force their way to the most strategic position – yet Jesus's eye is caught by the cripple of 38 years, quite likely half obscured and trampled on by the press of the crowd. He has no hope of being cured. And Jesus asks him, 'Do you want to be healed?' He is not going to do it to him but he respects his personal integrity and asks him to be a partner in the healing. And because Jesus has given him a sense of his own worth, has trusted him to be an agent in his own healing, so he is made whole and carries away the bed which for 38 years has carried him.

My last little scenario involves the man who was blind from birth. This is described in John's ninth chapter. The fact of his congenital blindness raised the question as to whether he or his parents had sinned, since an affliction of this sort was believed to be brought on by sin. Jesus makes a salve from the earth to put on the man's eyes and sends him off to wash in a well-known pool. When the lawyers get to hear of this they are extremely anxious and seek to blacken Jesus's reputation in the eyes of those who are disposed to admire him, by calling him a troublemaker who is leading the people away from God ... and how little has changed in the intervening years. 'What are Jesus's credentials? Where does he come from? Has he been to the right university? Why haven't we heard of him?' And then comes the telling put-down and it takes the experience of the person healed to cut through all the pious talk and come out with:

The man answered, 'Now, that is remarkable! You don't know where he comes from, yet he opened my eyes. We know that God does not listen to sinners. He listens to the godly man who does his will.'

'Nobody has ever heard of opening the eyes of a man born blind. If this man were not from God he could do nothing.'

To this the Pharisees replied, 'You were steeped in sin at birth: how dare you lecture us?' And they threw him out. Jesus heard that they had thrown him out and when he found him, he said, 'Do you believe in the Son of Man?'

'Who is he, Sir?' the man asked. 'Tell me so that I may believe in him.'

Jesus said, 'You have now seen him: in fact, he is the one speaking with you.'

These are wonderful human stories, with glimpses of Jesus' humour and teasing and scolding and compassion. Years later I came to realize something about Jesus and all the people with whom he came into contact, and that was this: whenever he was faced with a situation in which he was presented with a choice between a relationship and an issue he always aligned himself with the relationship at the expense of the issue, even at the risk of being misunderstood. When the woman caught in the act of adultery was exposed she was clearly surrounded by a hostile group of people. Jesus was being set up and tested on one of the Ten Commandments, which he had to endorse. And yet he put himself against the accusers and therefore with the accused by his direction that, 'He who is without sin should cast the first stone.' And when they have all gone away – the eldest first – he says, 'Does no one condemn you? Then neither do I, but go and sin no more'.

That 'Neither do I' was what the Pharisees heard, and having heard it their ears were closed to the 'Go and sin no more'.

In that act – as in so many others – he demonstrated that our world is one in which we are all equal under God and that we all, because of our humanity, share in the world's imperfections and in the propensity to go our own way without ensuring that we are online with God.

Now the traditional view of official Christianity has viewed the world as one which was tainted with sin and imperfection as a result of the disobedience of Adam and the ensuing corruption of not only the human race but of the whole of God's Creation. In its more extreme form the world is seen as doomed unless individuals and parts of creation are redeemed by coming under the rule of God – that only in Christ can one be in a relationship with God, and this thinking has informed so much of the understanding and teaching of the church. In this atmosphere it almost inevitably meant that a morbid view of the human condition developed and that there was an overdeveloped sense of guilt, both collectively and individually. Great value was put on acts of self-denial and on ascetic lifestyles: in extreme cases individuals would be expelled from the church and only allowed back after significant repentance and acts of restitution.

Not surprisingly, there have been many down the ages who have reacted negatively to these excesses and either they have left the church or they have developed a theology of righteousness which has led to their having no need for repentance.

But a positive view of human value and a strong sense of sin are by no means incompatible, as we can see in our encounters with Jesus in the Gospels. When Jesus made contact with those to whom he ministered he did so on the basis of a complete empathy with them and a sense – on the other side – of someone who valued them and whose transparent goodness made them only too well aware of their own failure to love or value others as he loved them.

So instead of a strong sense of guilt and a negative view of self, the true penitent sees his situation as full of hope and faith in Christ's forgiveness and a great need for the renewal and healing which he brings.

But all this took place in a society where many of its leaders saw the human race not as one body valued by God – and in need of his forgiveness and renewal – but as a society which claimed God's favour and sought to keep itself uncontaminated by those who were not part of the chosen race, and whose lives of impurity and law-breaking had separated them from God.

So in order for them to be able to discern between those who were and were not of God there gradually grew up a tradition of detailed interpretation of the law in which practically every situation was catered for, and those which weren't could be sorted out by the local rabbi. In effect the law seemed to encourage people to think in terms of a pass mark culture. The perfection of God was 100 per cent. Then there was the law – the original Ten Commandments – and the details could be filled in by reference to the Torah (the first five books of our Old Testament). But in order to bring the law up to date and relevant to the lives of first-century Jews there had to be further interpretation in the form of an oral tradition whose guardians and teachers were the scribes and the rabbis – many of whom would be members of the Pharisee party, a renewal movement which grew up at a time of nationalist unrest provoked by first Greek and then Roman domination. It was a call back to the original covenant, when Israel promised to obey the law in return for God's protection and provision.

And this interpretation of the law was essentially practical. It was interpreted in such a way that the law could be kept, if not in practice, then as a realistic goal to be achieved. In just such a way pass marks in our own society are set as reasonable objectives. Our achievements in relation to such standards depends on where we come in the class list. Those of us who manage to pass are given a self-confidence which makes us comfortable: those who just fail are encouraged to make a special effort to score more. But there are those whose remarkable success persuades them that they are rather special: by the same token there are those who fail so abysmally that they don't even bother to try, and write themselves off – and may well be written off – from membership of the community.

Now Jesus was not anti-law: in fact he said that not one 'jot or tittle' of the law would pass away. He said that in relation to the law we all had to be far better than the scribes and Pharisees; that breaking the law started in the heart and in the mind before ever it reached people's behaviour. Indeed, it is not beyond the bounds of probability that Jesus was himself a member of the Pharisaic party. For, by and large, the Pharisees were really respected and made a great contribution to the religious life of the community. Let us remind ourselves of the Gospel references which comment on the division within the Pharisees about Jesus, and those such as Nicodemus and Joseph of Arimathea, who were clearly his disciples. What Jesus sought to do was to put the law back into a framework that would enable society to be focused on God but avoid the tendency to set people against each other and cause divisions rather than integration.

So in terms of the pass mark culture God becomes for Jesus not 100 per cent but infinitely good: that beside him and his love even the most outstandingly moral person scores less than 1 per cent, which means (so long as we are not distracted by the contradiction within the metaphor) all humans are effectively on the same level. What really decides our standing before God is not how far up the list we are but whether we are facing God or not and therefore whether we see his arms open wide for us, inviting us to continue on our journey and promising its successful conclusion.

And here was Jesus gathering more and more followers, and his words and actions seemed to be directed towards the destruction of the law and thereby the disintegration of the Jewish people. He was the last thing that they needed at a time when they were smarting under the Roman yoke and when their faith had already been corrupted by the dominance of Greek culture. Those, therefore, who looked at their fellow Jews and deplored the moral and religious backsliding which had reduced God's chosen people to such ignominy saw Jesus as a real threat to their worthy aims. They were supported in their opposition to him by those who were using religion and morals to boost their self-righteousness.

And so as Jesus exposed the law for the increasingly superficial and insensitive tool that (in some people's hands) it had become, so its guardians increasingly felt that he was a danger to the whole culture and the moral basis on which it stood. Anarchy was waiting in the wings – or so they feared – and with anarchy the threat of draconian steps to destroy it by the Romans.

So it dawned on the Jewish council that Jesus had to be got rid of, but his popularity was a problem – but as time went on measured thinking was supplanted by panic, a kangaroo court was convened and he was handed over to the Roman authorities. Yet he could have escaped. He needn't have gone to Jerusalem at a sensitive time when the Romans were half expecting trouble. Yet not to have done so would have put off the inevitable showdown between the protagonists.

Caiaphas summed it up when he said that it was better for one man to die than that the whole nation be destroyed. But he was thinking, really, of that particular community within that particular superstate at that particular period of time.

For Jesus, however, the stage was altogether greater and

more universally critical. All societies need the rule of law. All societies have to recognize that we live in the interim between the beginnings of creation and the end of time. But Jesus is the one who – more than any other – saw creation as developing the complete integration of the system which even we in the new millennium can only perceive dimly. Jesus knew that the principles of love, of shalom, of inter-relationship, of interaction, of inclusiveness – which we find in God and which are mirrored in Jesus's life – are the crucial principles by which any law stands or falls. That is why Jesus went to Jerusalem in such a calculated way. Not only was he convinced that this showdown had to take place, but that it should be enacted at a highly symbolic time – Passover – and place – Jerusalem.

Chapter 3

EASTER

I write this just after Easter when the events which followed on from Jesus' arrest and trial unfolded. The crucifixion – that calculated public display of execution, drawn out over hours in order to maximize the deterrent value of the sentence; the burial in the tomb of a member of the Sanhedrin (?); the mystery and the reality of the Resurrection.

And the question is asked again – why did Jesus die? And we have heard so many answers – often the clichés which we have picked up from church, or from school assemblies or religious studies courses. Jesus died to save us from our sins. Jesus died to show us that he has won the victory over death. Jesus died because God needed to be paid for our sins, so Jesus took our place and sacrificed himself for us. All can make some sense in the proper context.

It is sometimes easier to answer a question like this more naively. Jesus died because he valued every human person, because he knew that God values every human as his creation, and therefore there is nothing that a human can do which would cancel God's love for them. They might estrange themselves from God through their guilt, but he, as the father of the prodigal son, is there, waiting for the prodigal to say: 'Father, I have sinned before you and am no longer worthy to be called your son.' And when he was still far off, the parable goes: 'his

33

father went to meet him and threw his arms around him.' And that sort of love is creative – it proliferates. It is exchanged between two people. It passes from one person to another, it enables the person loved to become more confident in themselves and therefore to be able to risk being themselves and giving themselves to others. And these others themselves become what God created them to be and the whole mechanism expands and grows exponentially.

Have you noticed that there are some people who can make a room full of people glow simply by their presence? They exude a warmth which rubs off on everyone and enhances the moment quite magically. How often has an unconfident schoolchild been taken to one side by a wise school teacher and told that their teacher has faith in them and knows that they can achieve the particular goal that is before them. Love brings new life to both the giver and the receiver.

Now this is all very well and theoretically marvellous, but our experience of people tells us that God gives each of us different gifts, and some people find it easier than others to relate to fellow humans. Some individuals, on the other hand, may not find it so easy to love their fellows in the conventional sense and are gifted with more academic, or more practical talents. But that does not mean that their capacity for love is any less. In their way, each of them can play their part in making a joined up world. In love the craftsman, or builder, or electrician can choose how conscientiously he does the job and, therefore, how well he enables those who live in the building he has serviced to be comfortable, or safe, or economical and so serve others better. In love the awkward, seemingly offhand, even selfish young academic can be so dedicated to her task of revealing the meaning and relevance of great works of literature to her readers that they gain greater insights into the minds of themselves and others.

Yet if we consider this seriously, we find ourselves feeling that there are categories of people who do not come within the compass of this exchange. Some people have so demonstrated that love is the antithesis of their relationships with other humans, that we find it impossible to accept that they would ever respond to our love; still less would they initiate it. To love others would demand so much from us that we feel that the price is too great to pay. Yet there is an inbuilt check within each one of us which says that whatever we give out, we should expect something in return, even if we have to wait forever. Sadly, we all know that our patience often gives out quite quickly.

And then we come across something like this. It comes from a little book, *Becoming Human* by Jean Vanier, in which he speaks of the experiences of caring for those with physical and mental handicaps, and of the l'Arche communities which were established for patients and carers. *"Antonio was one member. He could not walk, speak, or use his hands. He needed extra oxygen to breathe. He was a weak and fragile man in many ways, but he had an incredible smile and beautiful shining eyes. There was no anger or depression in him. The only love that Antonio could give was a love of trust. But Antonio touched and wakened the hearts of many assistants who came to live in his house. He led them into the way of the heart. Often they would say, in words to this effect; "Antonio has changed my life. He led me out of a society of competition where one has to be strong and aggressive into a world of tenderness and mutuality, where each person strong or weak, can exercise their gifts."*

The Dutch priest and writer, Henry Nouwen, who worked in one of the l'Arche communities, said this in his book, Adam, which describes his contact with a man who had severe physical and intellectual disabilities.

"Here is the man who more than anyone connected me with my inner self, my community and my God. Here is the man I was asked to care for, but who took me into his life and his heart in such an incredibly deep way. Here is my counsellor, my teacher, my guide, who could never say a word to me but taught me more than any book, professor or spiritual director."

≡≡

Very late in my teens I started to take Rugby seriously. There were no leagues or cups in those days, though our fixture list was one of the strongest and meant that there were few easy games. Perhaps the biggest challenge, therefore, was our annual Easter Tour to South Wales. And perhaps for the first time, I found myself knowingly being out of step with the majority of those I was with.

We started by playing Bath on Maundy Thursday evening. On Good Friday we travelled by road to Swansea, in those days a very run down place, and were put up in a commercial hotel in the High Street: a rather dismal establishment which did not encourage us to behave in the gentlemanly and civilized way which is the hallmark of Rugby tours! We always had a good game against Swansea; good rugby was appreciated and the hospitality was generous... which meant that when Easter Sunday morning came round, there was just three or four of us who walked a few yards up the street to the Anglican Church to receive communion, before driving to the Gower Peninsular to join the rest in playing the annual game of golf for the Harlequin Cup. Easter Monday was the toughest day for we had to drive all the way to Cardiff and the strength of their team at the time meant that we invariably got beaten.

Looking back at those days, my faith was in Jesus of the Bible. My commitment to the church was through those who had nurtured my faith; my Cambridge College, where as a choral scholar I had to sing services in the Chapel, the young woman whose faith challenged me to read the Bible, and who subsequently (surprise, surprise!) became my wife. But I accepted the Resurrection as part and parcel of the package, and my assent to it was really only a token of my commitment to Jesus and the church. Looking back, I believe that there were two reasons for this. The first was that books I was reading as I sought to know more and more about my faith, seemed to be written with a view to setting out a logical argument to account for the recorded phenomena. Because I was hooked, so to speak, without analyzing the arguments too carefully, I was prepared to accept that the physical resurrection of Jesus was proved, in spite of the difficulties presented by the descriptions of some of the appearances. The second was that I had not yet learnt that Christianity, unlike the other two monotheistic faiths, Judaism and Islam, is a religion of grace and not a religion of effort. So I was easily persuaded that by my own efforts I could prove to others that I had become a Christian, by the way I behaved, and I had little real conception of the relationship between the risen Christ and the work of the Holy Spirit.

While rugby careers are relatively short lived, it took me a long time to begin to appreciate the deeper meaning of the Passion. While the church that we attended was a wonderfully active fellowship, with a tremendous sense of our obligation to God and to the community, in common with many other evangelical churches, it lacked any real liturgical imagination, because it was so tied to the written word. So it wasn't until I responded to a need for youth work leadership in one of the other churches in the town that we were introduced to a more sacramental approach to the Easter story. While the Good Friday liturgy was still somewhat wordy, we began to understand the concept of Vigil and the freshness and wonder of the first Eucharist of Easter as the sun rose over the adjacent River Thames.

Yet, if I am honest, the Resurrection still left me with what I have called the 'so what' factor. My faith has nothing to do with the ability of anyone to do conjuring tricks. It leaves me absolutely cold. I am too well aware that what passes as a miracle to some is easily accounted for by recorded phenomena well known to geologists, astronomers, doctors or other experts. I also understand that scientific laws are only arrived at by the measurement of statistical means, and an isolated aberration at a given scale might, at a much larger scale, be shown to be a regular occurrence.

So it is quite possible that the walls of Jericho were subject to a seismic shock in a region well known for such occurrences; that when God spoke to Moses out of the burning bush, he was witnessing a fairly common phenomenon, whereby some desert thorn bushes do spontaneously combust in the heat of the day, but adapted as they are to severe drought they survive by dint of their very tough branches, and it is only the leaves which catch fire; that when the Red Sea opened up to allow the Israelites to pass over, and then caught the Egyptian chariots as the water returned, they were witnessing a natural event whereby a shallow area in the region was made passable by the force of "a strong east wind".

Now I have said elsewhere that it does seem clear that, nonetheless, God is a God who intervenes in history. But that is a very different thing to claiming that he regularly and arbitrarily appears to contravene scientific principles to send his children running instructions as it were. I remember a young colleague of mine recounting his experience on a Christian holiday camp, where the caterer was clearly a rather feckless young man who had forgotten to order meat for forty people's Sunday lunch. They were extremely fortunate that they were near enough to an abattoir which happened to be open very late at night, and they ascribed their good fortune to a miracle. 'Thank you, Lord' was the prayer, 'for finding us some meat'! My colleague cited this as one of the reasons why he (temporarily) gave up on church.

I have always found William Temple's approach to miracles a great help. In his Readings in St John's Gospel, he says that we should have no problem with the creator: God's ability to do what he likes with his own creation. But we then have to ask ourselves whether, in the light of what we know about Jesus, the priorities which he made for himself and his refusal to advertise his powers, some of his miracles, perhaps, owe more to the need for the early church to express their beliefs about Jesus than to objective scientific observation.

Perhaps Jesus himself gave us the best criteria for judging the accounts of his work. The very first thing that he did after he had been baptized by John was to take himself off into the wilderness to be tempted by Satan. His temptations were significant. He could have taken the role of the great provider, and in an area impoverished by the demands of their imperial overlords, there would have been great support for such a wonder worker. He could have shown himself to be far above the human frailties and weaknesses to which he had come to minister and thereby claimed every mortal's allegiance. He could have raised up an army of national liberation to complete the work of the Maccabbean resistance movement and reclaim Judaea for God's own people.

Yet he resisted all these and chose instead the way of self sacrificial love. Unobtrusive, unsentimental, realistic love which sought the cooperation of those in need, and respected their integrity as fellow children of God; his own brothers and sisters. And even then he was by no means unique as a healer and wonder worker, for there are many well recorded instances of other men with healing powers. Jesus was just one among many at that time and in that region.

But all this assumes that we are the ones who listen all the time and God occasionally favours us with his direction. But it is quite the other way round, for we are the ones whose ears are only tuned from time to time, while God too often has to wait for us to take any notice of him. Crucially, I believe, God's way of speaking to us in miracles, or signs as John significantly calls them, is a matter of timing. Often we are subconsciously aware of a particular concern or anxiety which is gnawing away, and a fairly straightforward phenomenon will coincide with our thoughts to suddenly give us a new idea or a certainty, or a great feeling of warmth, or even a vision or a spoken word. I particularly like the story of Elijah where he hears God speaking through a 'still, small voice'.

But to return to the Resurrection; through chance, and through personal inclination, we found ourselves in churches which were more catholic in their approach to liturgy and, to a lesser extent, theology. But what did stand out was a completely different approach to worship. At last, Holy Week and Easter really stood out as the Festival of the whole year, the calendar of the liturgical year gave a rhythm to worship which had always been lacking in other churches, tied as they were to evangelistic campaigns and courses of study, and I began to realise the simplicity and profundity of the Sacrament of the Mass as the focus of the liturgy brought it centre stage.

There was one particular year when the amateur choir to which I belonged was preparing to give a performance of Bach's St Matthew Passion in the largest church in our immediate neighbourhood. The soloists, orchestra and conductor were all professionals, and three rehearsals were planned in the final week, with the performance on the Saturday before Palm Sunday. By Saturday afternoon, I was exhausted. With Palm Sunday, Holy Week and then the Easter services I did not know how I was going to cope. In the event, the performance was extremely moving and the Passion provided the perfect prologue to the next week's devotions. Instead of being exhausted I was on a high, which lasted for the whole of Holy Week.

Intellectually, however, I was little nearer to an appreciation of the Easter event than I had been before. But during this time of parish ministry, I was able to share in another side of death and resurrection. Perhaps the greatest privilege that came to me was that of ministering to those who were near death and to those whom they left behind. Their different reactions were quite unpredictable and often surprising, and with very few exceptions, I came away with positive sentiments

I suspect that some of the doubts which I noticed had to do with the traditional belief, summed up in the 16th verse of the third chapter of John's Gospel, and pronounced every Sunday in the 'comfortable words' which precede the confession and absolution in the Communion Service – "God so loved the world, that he gave his only begotten Son, that whosoever believeth in Him should not perish but have everlasting life." – and so often interpreted as a death sentence on any who, for whatever reason, could not confidently recite the Creed. The story of the Rich man (Dives) and Lazarus also helps to suggest that unless we accept the Christian Faith in this life, then we have no hope of getting to heaven.

Yet my encounter with those who were bereaved, and my own understanding of the Bible, have made me more and more convinced that real life is all about the creative interaction of human individuals with each other and with the whole of the rest of God's creation. Time and time again I heard people speak of their lost loved one in terms of the effect they had on people's lives and the vivid recollections which helped to lift the gloom of bereavement.

One of my more frustrating encounters was a visit I was asked to make to the house of a non-churchgoer who was anxious to see a priest. He was a director of one of the biggest public utilities in the UK and he wanted to talk about what he called the 'fourth dimension'. I saw him twice, and we talked for as long as he could physically manage, and in that short time we 'clicked' and seemed to cover far more ground than the actual time would suggest. Within the week he was dead. I took the funeral, and was invited to the 'wake' in a local hotel. The service in which one of his friends gave a eulogy and my conversations with his friends and associates at the reception revealed what a real ministry he had had as a manager. One man, describing his interview for a job, said he came out of the room 'feeling that he had been hugged', and one after another people I heard talk about their boss as someone who instead of wielding power from above, led from alongside, and encouraged people to feel that they were valued and could do a good job. It was only later that I found out that he was a great rugby person, had captained his University and maintained an active and creative interest ever since. Perhaps there was a good reason for my ignorance about this, for we might still have been talking Rugby even if he had survived for twice the time I knew him!

And I can think of so many people whose lives and deaths together have called to mind the words of John the Evangelist in the first chapter – "In him was life, and that life was the light of men".

Who? A priest in inner-city Birmingham who died at the age of 47, leaving her husband and two little girls, correcting someone who described her as 'dying of cancer' with 'No, I am <u>living with cancer</u>.' And what a moving yet utterly joyful funeral she had, led by many in the afro-Caribbean congregation, taking it in turns with the shovel to completely fill in the grave, with a choir singing impromptu what I can only describe as music of light and life.

A young mother of four whose husband aged 41, died suddenly in front of the television one Boxing Day evening when all the family had gone to bed; the two hundred and fifty people who came to the funeral; the quiet dignity of the family in church, and the return to church of mother who was baptized and confirmed eighteen months later – all of this a marvellous example of what I can only call positive sadness.

A family whose baby had revealed symptoms of heart disease from the age of ten days, which afflicted him till he died on the operating table on Maundy Thursday eighteen months later. Mother deeply committed to the church, father not a churchgoer, but happy to be involved in the life of the church community, responding to their bereavement in very positive ways and delighting in the gift of another son. All these are living examples of a remark I picked up from an Oxford theologian – 'wherever you draw the line, you will always find Jesus on the other side.'

And finally, two very personal revelations. I have always had a fear of death, and have suffered from varying degrees of depression in adulthood. Yet I had one very strong realisation when I was sitting up in bed one morning. I was thinking of my children and the full lives the three of them were living, and as parents often do, experiencing a moment of real pride in the way they lived their lives, and particularly their talent for relationships with others. I suddenly realised that what happened to me from then on did not really matter, because I was utterly bound up in them in lots of very different ways. And by extension, the same was true: a propos of all the other relationships which I had been able to make with people beyond the boundaries of my own family. This gave me a deep sense of peace, and while the intensity of that sensation has not been repeated, its memory goes some way to open up the concept of resurrection.

The second is much easier to revisit since the opportunities present themselves over and over again. We are fortunate to belong to a large extended family which has its physical focus in a large house in the west of Scotland. The occasion I particularly recall was a supper party for thirty at New Year. It consisted of Granny and then a pyramid of relationships which reached down to third cousins and across to friends, friends' friends, and casual acquaintances. This was a reflection on the hospitality of the hosts and their ministry to 'all sorts and conditions' of humanity. Some were wealthy, some impecunious, some upright members of the community, some more than down on their luck. Some were quietly self-confident, some noisily inadequate. Yet we were all linked with everyone else in relationship, and as each began to sense the atmosphere of acceptance and welcome, so they were able to feel valued and therefore set free to be themselves and to discard, even if only just a little, the defensive shield with which they concealed and protected their true selves. And inasmuch as this happened to each one, so there was a resurrection happening individually and corporately.

And as I look back on that particular scene and experience similar ones, though never since on that scale, so I realise that I have had a glimpse of the Kingdom of God and the new risen life which we have in Jesus. No wonder he drew attention to that last supper that he had with his disciples and gave us that memorial.

I have said as much as I can about the Resurrection. As a priest, and particularly as a Parish vicar, I have to balance my own experience with the creeds which I have affirmed, and the vows that I made at my ordination. But let us remind ourselves of that little story of Blondin and Niagara Falls. The only real proof of our faith is the degree to which it is reflected in our actions. Jesus said, "If anyone would come after me, he must deny himself and take up his cross and follow me. For whoever wants to save his life will lose it, but whoever loses his life for me will find it." New, risen life indeed.

Chapter 4

AND THEN WHAT?

It would be nice, but totally unreal, if the rest of the Christ story recounted life that was lived on the level of the resurrection experiences that I have recounted and others which were, more or less, intense and prolonged. One can easily imagine the very varied feelings which Jesus' followers experienced. Some would be waiting in confident expectation of something happening, and others would be depressed by a sense of anticlimax and disappointment. Yet one thing was clear and that was that the disciples were 'all together'. And as I reread that story in the second chapter of Acts, I find myself trying to retranslate the story into a reality that I can recognize as authentic, without ignoring the fact that the event was centred on the Spirit of God.

I feel that in the early church's experience there is a great deal of waiting.

First Jesus is crucified and then a couple of days later he is seen by some of his disciples – but not by them all. Thomas has to wait another week before he is able to say – 'My Lord and my God!' and he does not appear to others until later still. Even then, as on the road to Emmaus, it takes time to recognize him and when they do he disappears again almost immediately. Similarly, at the Ascension a few days later, the disciples go to meet him on the mountain and a cloud removes him from their sight; and then they have to wait again and we come to this amazing experience at the feast of Pentecost, when traditionally the Jews celebrated the giving of the Law.

"When the day of Pentecost came, they were all together in one place. Suddenly a sound like the blowing of a violent wind came from heaven and filled the whole house where they were sitting. They saw what seemed to be tongues of fire that separated and came to rest on each of them. All of them were filled with the Holy Spirit and began to speak in other tongues as the Spirit enabled them. Now there were, staying in Jerusalem, God-fearing Jews from every nation under heaven. When they heard this sound, a crowd came together in bewilderment, because each one heard them speaking in his own language. Utterly amazed, they asked: "Are not all these men who are speaking Galileans? Then how is it that each of us hears them in his own native language? Parthians, Medes and Elamites; residents of Mesopotamia, Judea and Cappadocia, Pontus and Asia, Phrygia and Pamphylia, Egypt and the parts of Libya near Cyrene; visitors from Rome (both Jews and converts to Judaism); Cretans and Arabs – we hear them declaring the wonders of God in our own tongues!" Amazed and perplexed, they asked one another, "What does this mean?" Some, however, made fun of them and said, "They have had too much wine." Then Peter stood up with the Eleven, raised his voice and addressed the crowd: "Fellow Jews and all of you who live in Jerusalem, let me explain this to you; listen carefully to what I say. These men are not drunk, as you suppose. It's only nine in the morning! No, this is what was spoken by the prophet Joel:

"'In the last days, God says, I will pour out my Spirit on all people. Your sons and daughters will prophesy, your young men will see visions, your old men will dream dreams.

And what an experience; first a noise like a strong driving wind, a stirring among those who met together, very powerful, but with no obvious agent to cause it. You see the results without being able to identify the cause.

Then tongues of flame over the assembled company. What can that have been? Perhaps if we translated that into 'catching alight' we get a better idea. We know how words, or for that matter music, or any of the arts which in one performance can seem utterly dead, can be transformed into a totally different experience in a performance which is inspired – there we are; its the same word again – breath or wind.

Finally, the disciples are understood by people of many different languages; somehow there is a basic harmony in the gathering which overcomes the barriers of language and culture.

Not only is this event a tremendous experience and change, but it is so unaccountable in terms of normal behaviour that the onlookers can only interpret it as drunkenness. And it doesn't stop there, because from then on the disciples are transformed from a demoralised group who meet behind closed doors for fear of the Jews, to a fellowship of people who fearlessly spread the good news no matter what it costs them.

How many of us remember learning to ride a bicycle, or how many have taught their children or grandchildren to do so? The technique, of course, is simple. You get on the bike, held by the adult, and you are told that to stay upright; all you have to do is to turn the handlebars in the direction that you feel you are falling. You start off and concentrate like mad, but of course you are immediately on the ground and have to start all over again. Sooner or later, you make your first few yards on your own and shortly after that you can pedal as well. It is not long before you are bowling along the footpath, terrorizing the old ladies and small dogs and children which obstruct your progress. And by this time you are so proficient that you no longer have to concentrate; you find yourself riding along by the light of nature and so fine the balance that the idea of 'turning into the direction you are falling' is irrelevant.

In this example the bicycle, which was an alien piece of technology which you had to master, has become an extension of yourself; a tool with which you are at one, and you proceed quite unconscious of the skill you have acquired.

One can extend this development through a myriad of other analogies. To master a musical instrument, and perform a difficult piece, one has to practice scales and exercises to attain an adequate technique and then observe all the dynamics and time directions to produce the performance.

But then we go to the concert hall and if we are lucky, we will hear something in which the instrument is simply an extension of the artiste, and the music speaks directly to us and we feel that composer, performer, and audience are all connected. The gulf between the earnest student and the inspired genius is colossal.

The skills of the professional sports person illustrate the same point. The Rugby player is taught to swerve, to sidestep, to dummy, to pass, to kick; and he is coached in making the correct decision at the appropriate moment of the game. Yet only when he does these things by the light of nature, and instinctively at the moment of best opportunity, will he prove successful, and those watching and playing with him will appreciate his talent.

After the crucifixion of Jesus, the disciples were rather like the amateur practitioners that I have described above. They were used to being instructed by their teacher; they knew what they should do. But it was a question of reproducing what they had seen Jesus do – and they were scared. 'The disciples were gathered together, for fear of the Jews' is one of the descriptions that we find in the Acts, and clearly they were struggling to fulfil the great commission.

The events of Pentecost record the watershed between this conscious following and repeating the effects of one who had gone before them, and suddenly (or not so suddenly) discovering that they had been given the inner and subconscious compulsion to be as he was – and now is – through them.

And, of course, it happened when they were all gathered together. The power of fellowship is so natural and universally experienced that it has become unremarkable, but it does highlight the importance of gathering with others to push forward a religious or political idea. And given the uniqueness of this particular occasion, we need not be surprised by the intensity of the experience for the gathered community and for those who were spectators. We must, of course, also take account of the totally different culture of the Middle East; not to mention a reminder that all this happened two thousand years ago. We often forget just how much we take our own cultural background as the baseline of our language and opinions.

But right up to the present generation, there has always been the temptation to emphasise the superficial and obvious at the expense of the more profound – if less spectacular. So a timely reminder of the sort of ministry that Jesus exercised is found at the end of the Acts, Chapter 2, where we read:

"Those who accepted his message were baptized, and about three thousand were added to their number that day. They devoted themselves to the apostles' teaching and to the fellowship, to the breaking of bread and to prayer. Everyone was filled with awe, and many wonders and miraculous signs were done by the apostles. All the

believers were together and had everything in common. Selling their possessions and goods, they gave to anyone as he had need. Every day they continued to meet together in the temple courts. They broke bread in their homes and ate together with glad and sincere hearts, praising God and enjoying the favor of all the people. And the Lord added to their number daily those who were being saved."

Yet even then the convention was that 'religion' was other worldly, and this had to be countered by teaching such as found in the parable of the sheep and the goats in Matthew 25:

"Then the righteous will answer him, 'Lord, when did we see you hungry and feed you, or thirsty and give you something to drink? When did we see you a stranger and invite you in, or needing clothes and clothe you? When did we see you sick or in prison and go to visit you?' "The King will reply, 'I tell you the truth, whatever you did for one of the least of these brothers of mine, you did for me.' "

And so to the theological statement – which comes from the First Letter of John:

"Dear friends, since God so loved us, we also ought to love one another. No one has ever seen God; but if we love one another, God lives in us and his love is made complete in us. We know that we live in him and he in us, because he has given us of his Spirit. And we have seen and testify that the Father has sent his Son to be the Saviour of the world. If anyone acknowledges that Jesus is the Son of God, God lives in him and he in God. And so we know and rely on the love God has for us. God is love. Whoever lives in love lives in God, and God in him."

The trouble with love is that it is not always recognizable, and we like to have a religion which produces results. For if we understand the work of God in creation, we know that it is about integration, that it involves an exchange in which each interacting part is made more perfect, more complete and this involves not only humans, but the whole creation. And the other problem is that love in human terms is terribly uneconomic, for it involves individuals giving to and receiving from other individuals.

My understanding of the Holy Spirit is inextricably bound up with the love that Jesus had for every human person, which showed itself in his self-sacrificial dealings with them. This love crystallized in his human form and life; the creative, holy spirit by which God brought the universe about and by which he still breathes life into it. And this Holy Spirit is embodied in a worldwide community of those who have responded to the love of Jesus and in their turn, they are living his life through their actions and ministry. They are the church, the Body of Christ – the human expression of those who are bound together by their allegiance to Jesus, still deeply flawed in their humanity, but at the same time empowered by the Holy Spirit to convey the truth about God through word and deed.

Chapter 5

THE WORD OF GOD?

I write this as someone who owes a tremendous amount to the Bible as one of the main means of leading me to faith. I have recounted elsewhere how I was led to read the Gospels and how I shared the same experience as J B Phillips in discovering in its pages the ring of truth. I was encouraged to use it as a manual for Christian living and to look for direct significance to my own life in every extract which I read. But I began to ask questions to which I did not find satisfactory answers.

I could not understand why there seemed to be so much emphasis on the writings of St Paul and so little on the Gospels. I was puzzled by the fact that someone (or a group of people) was responsible for the choice of the Old and New Testament writings which made them, rather than the Bible, the final authority.

I was rather lucky in that the beginnings of my interest in the Bible coincided almost exactly with the publication of the New Testament of the New English Bible. I was – and still am – in no position to evaluate this translation in comparison with others but I found it down to earth and plain speaking and that it brought Jesus and the other characters to life, so that their humanity was emphasized as never before. To turn back to the Authorized Version proved in these circumstances to spoil the picture and to distance me from the reality of the personalities.

When I came to the writings of St Paul, however, I had rather more difficulty. I could accept that here was a very gifted person, but he was one who came from a completely different culture – one in which the tradition of sacrifice as appeasement of God for wrongdoing (even as payment of a fine) simply didn't resonate with me and – I suspect – with many others of my generation, at least. I found St Paul to be too authoritarian and to reflect the customs of the age and community in which he lived. His strictures against women, particularly, ran contrary to my family tradition and beliefs and his writings – while instructive – could not have the authority of the Gospels, so far as I was concerned.

Yet the impression that I got from some quarters was that St Paul's writings dictated what one should believe almost more than the Gospels.

It was not until I began to train for the ordination that I began to see how things slotted into place. Perhaps the thing that particularly excited me was the opening up of the Old Testament. In the first place, I hardly knew anything of it. I had a basic knowledge of some of the main stories, such as Abraham, Moses, David, Solomon etc. but I was very aware that the God that we met in the Old Testament was certainly not the God whose incarnation was Jesus Christ. Here was a crude, violent, judgemental God who seemed to epitomize all the worst characteristics of the power of the universe.

But my guided tour combined the findings of Biblical scholars over a long period of time, the corroboration of the more recent discoveries of archaeology and my own background as a geographer involving the early cultures of the Fertile Crescent – as well as the climatological and geological succession of that area.

I have traced the origins of the creation stories in a previous chapter: the realization that these were stories which were the authors' attempts to convey what they believed about the relationship of the constituent parts of the earth with their one creator gave them a power and reality which authenticated their message in a way which a more literalistic meaning simply could not achieve.

An examination of the story of Noah and the Flood was similarly eye-opening. For some time I had been using a history of scientific discoveries book as a background to teaching basic geology to sixth-formers. The particular one relevant to the Flood was about the researches of Sir Leonard Woolley in the valleys of the Tigris and the Euphrates. He had been digging through the succession of silt layers and was gradually uncovering evidence of different cultures whose development was regularly interrupted by floods, as suggested by the absence of artefacts at various levels. The archaeologists had finally reached a level beyond which there seemed to be uninterrupted silt. They were at the point of giving up – having cut down through many feet without finding anything – when they suddenly came across further artefacts, quite different to anything that had gone before. They were puzzling over this when Lady Woolley surveyed the scene and said, 'It's the Flood – Noah's Flood.'

Now the timescale of all this is inevitably sketchy. We are talking about stories handed down by an oral tradition, of which the Noah version is only one. There is another, which concerns one Utnapishtim (which we outlined in the first chapter, and noted the uncanny resemblance to the Noah version) but the differences between them – the one God of Noah, and the multiplicity of Utnapishtim's; the moral basis of Noah's Flood and the arbitrary nature of the other – reveal the different religious cultures of the region of that time and the beginnings of the Jews' unique place within it.

But even more exciting to me was the fact that, broadly

speaking BCE, the timescale suggested that this event coincided with the glacial optimum of a few thousand years when evidence all over the northern hemisphere points to a significantly warmer climate and – as a result – a sea level of about four metres higher than at present. These two factors combined would mean higher rainfall in the catchment areas of the rivers concerned, along with greater flooding due to the higher base level and the resultant decrease in gradient.

Other examples of relevant physical phenomena come to mind. There is the story of the walls of Jericho collapsing so that Joshua could raise a siege and take the city. This was in an area on the fringes of the Mediterranean, where the African tectonic plate is pushing into the Eurasian one to the north. The resultant subduction of the African plate under the Eurasian one is accompanied by shock waves due to the friction caused and the destruction of any edifices which lie in their path.

The accompanying volcanic activity also has New Testament connections such as the phenomenon of the Pool of Siloam, whose regular disturbance was the signal for those suffering from illnesses severe or minor to plunge into the water in the expectation of a cure. Though, of course, the most celebrated healing associated with this site was Jesus's ministry to the man who had been a cripple for 38 years and had been unable to reach the water.

I have so far recorded some of the eye-openers that came to me in my study of the Bible. More generally, I realised that the Old Testament gradually became the story of a community from its very small beginnings in a group of pastoral nomads to the establishment of a significant political force in a strategic position in the Fertile Crescent. The different sources of the stories which made up the books served to create a multi-dimensional picture in which the dominant theme was the interaction of the one and only God with a people who recognized him but who struggled against their natural desire to control their own destiny without losing his protection. Their journey over what probably amounts to about 2,000 years ranges from the pinnacle of success achieved by David and enjoyed by his son Solomon contrasting with the ignominy of the destruction of Jerusalem and the exile to Babylon – and the subsequent humiliation by the Greek and Roman Empires. As a result, later writings – notably the prophet Isaiah – approach things from a more spiritual rather than a political angle and we perceive – though admittedly in hindsight – a link to the very different teaching and emphasis of Jesus.

More or less standing on their own we have the 150 Psalms, poems of very varying moods and style – of praise, of despair, of triumph and humility. Above all they are intensely human, revealing people in their worst and in their best moments. By turns vengeful and contrite, joyous and despairing, they convey the whole spectrum of human experience and because of that have become – almost more than any other part of the Bible – a basis for private devotions.

I think that it is appropriate to reproduce just one Psalm in its entirety to illustrate these poetic gems.

Psalm 139:
1 *O Lord, you have searched me and you know me.*
2 *You know when I sit and when I rise; you perceive my thoughts from afar.*
3 *You discern my going out and my lying down; you are familiar with all my ways.*
4 *Before a word is on my tongue you know it completely, O Lord.*
5 *You hem me in behind and before; you have laid your hand upon me.*

6 Such knowledge is too wonderful for me, too lofty for me to attain.

7 Where can I go from your Spirit? Where can I flee from your presence?

8 If I go up to the heavens, you are there; if I make my bed in the depths, you are there.

9 If I rise on the wings of the dawn, if I settle on the far side of the sea,

10 Even there your hand will guide me, your right hand will hold me fast.

11 If I say, 'Surely the darkness will hide me and the light become night around me.'

12 Even the darkness will not be dark to you; the night will shine like the day, for darkness is as light to you.

13 For you created my inmost being; you knit me together in my mother's womb.

14 I praise you because I am fearfully and wonderfully made; your works are wonderful, I know that full well.

15 My frame was not hidden from you when I was made in the secret place. When I was woven together in the depths of the earth...

16 Your eyes saw my unformed body. All the days ordained for me were written in your book before one of them came to be.

17 How precious to me are your thoughts, O God! How vast is the sum of them!

18 Were I to count them they would outnumber the grains of sand. When I awake, I am still with you.

19 If only you would slay the wicked, O God! Away from me, you bloodthirsty men!

20 They speak of you with evil intent; your adversaries misuse your name.

21 *Do I not hate those who hate you, O Lord, and abhor those who rise up against you?*

22 *I have nothing but hatred for them; I count them my enemies.*

23 *Search me, O God, and know my heart; test me and know my anxious thoughts.*

24 *See if there is any offensive way in me, and lead me in the way everlasting.*

With the advent of Jesus of Nazareth we come to a completely different type of writing. The impact that he gradually made was such that it is very difficult to disentangle what could be described as objective reporting and very subjective eulogy. It was quite likely not until the destruction of Jerusalem by the Romans and the persecution of Christians that Jesus's followers started to write down an account of their memories and their evaluation of this remarkable man. What stands out about the Gospels is that they record not only the life and ministry of Jesus but also what people believed about him, so that quite often it is impossible to disentangle historical accuracy and allegorical descriptions. It is not very surprising, however, that someone we have come to believe was the incarnate Son of God will be perceived as either too human or too God-like.

Of the two I think the greater danger is the latter. The belief that Jesus was the Son of God was largely a post-Resurrection belief. The disciples and the other followers of Jesus – during his own lifetime – knew him as their own friend and also as a friend of sinners. If St Peter did recognize the truth of Jesus in his confession at Caesarea Philippi it was probably just a momentary flash of inspiration and nowhere near the systematic theology which we hear in our creeds. From my own point of view he is intensely human, so much so that I am not really interested in whether he had never sinned (and on whose criterion of sin do we base this claim? That of the Pharisees? The man in the street? The national consensus?) I can't help feeling that the claim that he was sinless is more of a statement of his divinity than an observable moral fact. What we do find in him is an identification with humans that is more total than it could possibly be with any other human being. He claimed the first place in the hearts of his friends by what he was to them all.

But we need to remember that the first things written after the death of Jesus were not the Gospels but some of the Epistles and particularly the work of the ex-Pharisee Paul. Paul is astonishing. He was gifted with a good mind, amazing energy and a single-minded goal of re-establishing the Jewish religion as the only way of restoring Israel to her former greatness. He had probably been taught by the famous Pharisaic teacher Gamaliel and it was his concern that the new movement led by Jesus of Nazareth (which seemed to be getting under way) was a serious threat not only to the rigorous interpretations of the law that the Pharisees taught but might also develop into a seditious movement against the Romans, with catastrophic results for the Jewish faith. If anyone was likely to keep the law for a year and a day – and so, as they believed, bring the Messiah back to his people – it was going to be someone like Paul. According to the book of Acts St Paul was at least supportive of the arrest, trial and stoning of Stephen (the first recorded martyr of the church). From there he obtained permission to persecute the Christians in Damascus and it was on that journey that he experienced a personal encounter with Jesus, which was as dramatic as it was sudden. Or was it?

The road to Damascus lay along the eastern coast of the Mediterranean Sea – an inland route would have required Paul to go through Samaria, which no self-respecting Jew would contemplate. The scenery along that road is rugged and the physical features owe much to the mountainous nature of the land and the limited and very seasonal rainfall. As a result there are dramatic slopes and gullies and weird rock formations, which more temperate areas do not have. But the area is also subject to quite violent storms when air masses – of markedly different content – mix.

The obsessive Paul has been expending his energy stamping out the Jesus movement and, as he watches the process, he is aware of the contrast between the Christians and himself. He feels uneasy that the more he keeps the law the more he finds true peace beyond his grasp, and yet – as he looks at the dying Stephen – he is struck by the freedom and inner peace he conveys, compared with the torment going on in Paul's mind.

So he sets off for Damascus – probably with a couple of Roman soldiers to guard against banditry – but he, the Jew, rides on a little apart. So his mind is undistracted by activity and his breakdown coincides with some meteorological phenomenon and in it he is confronted, not by those whom he has persecuted, but by Jesus himself – whom he has never met – yet whom he now realizes that he knows through those who have so obviously appropriated his spirit.

And from that moment onwards, though not at first with much enthusiasm from the church, the energies which he had been devoting to the destruction of the church are now directed towards its support and extension.

We can trace Paul's progress through the Letters that he wrote to the various places around the Mediterranean and – through the account by his companion Luke in Acts – of the events and dangers that he encountered on his travels. He has two great themes. First, he is desperate to convey his experience of the inadequacy of simply keeping the law in all its detail. So clearly does he see that no matter how successful his efforts seem to be the gap between him and God is as great as ever. This is slavery to him for, by comparison with when he was forced – almost against his will – to acknowledge Jesus on the road to Damascus he gained a sense of the very freedom that he needed. His great urge is to convince other Jews of his experience and he travels round to the communities of the Jewish diaspora in the Mediterranean on this mission.

The second purpose that consumes him derives from his new-found release from the law. If – as a Jew – it was his inheritance from Abraham and the keeping of the law which put him right with God, now that he has recognized the law's enslavement it follows that Gentiles as well as Jews can be in the right relationship with God. This was a huge departure from the Jewish tradition and caused a serious rift in the young church, in which the original disciples and friends of Jesus stoutly defended the Jewishness of the church while Paul – with various friends – embarked upon their mission to the Gentiles.

But, in all this, Paul remained Paul. The Acts and the Letters show him to be the same person who was so proactive for the Jewish tradition. He had the same energy, the same self-confidence, the same tendency to think that he was right, and he brought a lot of the Pharisees with him. He was a first-century Turkish Jew through and through, yet one whom the risen Jesus was gradually transforming. We cannot understand Paul's message unless we hear it in the context of his Jewishness, his Middle Eastern culture and the time in which he lived. We cannot simply translate his theological and ethical exhortations into a 20th century western European milieu.

It is very important therefore that Paul's writings are

balanced by other letters and teachings of the time. Most particularly, the three Letters of John present a very different outlook in the church and contrast markedly with Paul. Finally the Revelation of St John concludes with a look into the future which is dominated by the political events of the moment (when so many experiencing the turmoil of the time were convinced that the world would end very soon).

We have looked at the various types of writing in the Bible and have run a critical eye over those parts which cause us problems. We have noted that texts and translations and contexts have a great role in conveying the true meaning of what the Bible says, and that not only the ideas of theologians but also the texts themselves have been added to as a result of new archaeological finds.

We can also discover that there are other writings from the same church period which find no place in the Bible and others again which are included in some versions and not in others, yet we know that the decisions to include or not were made by human beings who were church members. How is it that they are right and others whose opinions did not count were ignored?

So how and in what sense can we say that the Bible is the word of God? When we looked at the story of Noah's Flood we noted the contrast between the Utnapishtim story and that of Noah. Our reaction was to say, 'That is what it's all about. It's about the relationship between one creator God and his Creation. A great new truth has been revealed.' What we don't say is, 'This and that bit of detail is scientifically impossible, therefore it is all rubbish.' Nor do we feel we have to say, 'Because God has given us a further revelation of himself it must be complete and comprehensively accurate.' If God uses sinful humans to reveal himself there must be aspects of the message which are flawed, misleading and incomplete.

Now it would be quite reasonable to think that after 2,000 years of the church there would be a consensus about just how the scriptures should be interpreted – but for one radical event.

As the medieval church developed its teaching and authority struggled to control its members as corruption – both political and economic – grew. The dissemination of the Bible took huge steps forward, first through the translation of its texts into the various languages of western Europe and second through the development of the printing press. This provided a powerful weapon against some of the more dubious practices of the church, particularly the dangerous relationship between alms-giving and the absolution for sins committed (famously challenged by Martin Luther).

The Bible was the means by which corruption was successfully attacked, and also faith could become very much more personal. This had not only religious but political implications and has become perhaps the most significant watershed in the history of the church. It's not too surprising that the Bible – for some – has occupied the position of the final authority in matters of faith, with the tendency to give its texts exaggerated importance, even to the extent of allowing every word to contain something of the truth of God…and so for some its composition took on the form of automatic writing, with the author simply the tool which God used. So the Bible – for some – is less a story of God's revelation of himself to human kind but more of a detailed instruction manual for every aspect of human endeavour. Every situation has a verse which is applicable, and invariably that application is direct and insensitive to context and culture.

It was when the disciples really knew Jesus as a human person that they met God in him. By just the same token it is when we read the Bible as the inspired but fumbling expression of human reactions and the understanding of God's revelation of himself that it really comes to life in a miraculous way.

That is why the Bible is at the heart of the Church's prayer and the Church's liturgy. But the Bible also has to be guarded for, just as it provided a defence against the abuses which had crept into the Church, so it is also capable of being abused by those who use it – often inadvertently – to express a partisan, even an individual interpretation, as the incontrovertible truth of God. It is not unheard of for some people to use a pin to choose a book or a verse of the Bible and take that as guidance as to God's will. Certainly that is not much different from the process by which the early Church chose the successor of Judas Iscariot (by drawing lots). But we assume that the modern techniques of CVs, interviews and psychological profiling are better guides than pure chance and we also suggest that the Holy Spirit can work more effectively through the minds and experiences of humans than through the lottery of chance.

The Church, therefore, must be the authority for the choice of scripture and the Church must be the guardian of the Bible's interpretation. Yet there must always be an acceptance that there should be those who cast a radical eye over that interpretation, and that truth has so often come from those on the outside rather than the Establishment.

To that end we accept the disciplines of the scheme of readings for the Church's year – the Revised Common Lectionary – which is one of the best ecumenical tools to be introduced in recent years. The monastic tradition of the Church has also given us the Daily Office which provides a short liturgy of Psalms, Bible readings and other verses for every morning and evening of the year in a three-yearly cycle. Since there are up to four readings a day it means that we can complete a very comprehensive study of the Bible over a period of three years. The great advantage of this system is that because of the tightness of its form we are taken through the readings, the verses and the prayers. In our best moments we can concentrate on the readings and really put ourselves into the prayers and the canticles. In our worst moments (when the last thing we want to do is read the Bible and pray, or when we have an important commitment very imminently, or we are crippled by worry or anger) as we mouth the words of the Office and find ourselves distracted in the readings we get a sense that somehow God has taken over and we are in some way carried through by God. It has been one of the greatest gifts to us during the whole of our professional Church ministry and – as we so often find ourselves thinking – I wish we had latched on to it many years previously.

Yet for all the benefits of the Bible it is not universally accessible to those who seek to know God, for the written word is only effective so far in conveying the truth of Christ. And the issues which are presented are very complex and subtle so that while the principles involved apply to all people from the oldest to the youngest and from the cleverest to the most simple, unless everyone is taught on an individual level there is no way that the Biblical message can be adequately conveyed to a mixed gathering.

It is fairly standard practice, however, that if you preach to the children in a mixed-age congregation the people who will draw the greatest benefit will be their parents – partly because they will understand without feeling insulted by the style of presentation.

Perhaps more importantly we have to face the fact that there are still very varied traditions of Biblical interpretation, which cause real divisions in the Church. Not so very many years ago the real enemy of one section of the Church was not the Devil, nor Pol Pot – the despot who ruled Cambodia by terror – but the Bishop of Durham. Some Christians were convinced that his utterances were destructive of faith in God, while others were grateful to him for deepening their faith. Unfortunately the existence of theological colleges with particular – even doctrinal – tendencies encourages students to confirm their prejudices rather than learn from others (who have different bases of understanding). The relatively recent emphasis of theological training in diocesan ordination courses catering for all persuasions has been a tremendous advance, and the opportunity to be challenged over one's own theological sacred cow is an essential part of the preparation for the priesthood.

One of the staff of our Church was a young woman who, having trained as a teacher, had worked for a short time in Africa as part of a mission project and returned to train as a full-time parish worker. After a few years of impressive ministry she decided to undertake further training to qualify for the diaconate and went to the local theological college. She went from there to be a curate in Slough but had to wait several years before she could be ordained as a priest. Her first training had been very Bible-based and she described the unifying factor of the community as being based on a shared doctrinal basis, with the basis for those doctrines being a particular interpretation of the scriptures. She said that when she went to her second college the situation was quite different. There (within the broad confines of the Church's creeds) one could be High Church, Low Church, liberal or conservative and also have a similarly diverse approach to the Bible. What bound people together was their compulsory attendance at the Holy Communion service. She described the contrast between the two and said that she had found the Biblical/doctrinal straightjacket to be very difficult and the

Eucharistic focus immensely liberating.

But a great deal has happened in the time since the Reformation and the dissemination of the Bible. The printed word has come to dominate our lives to such an extent that much of what is published and certainly most of what is printed is lost on its recipients. How many of us have gone to pick up the post and automatically binned at least half of it? How many of us have received an insurance policy and have failed to read even half of its small print conditions?

And, not surprisingly, the Church has reflected this trend only too well. In the years that I have been in the Church we have had series one, two and three of the modern prayer book organized and particular religion they begat the Alternative Service Book 1980 and its cousins the books for Lent Holy Week and Easter and The Promise of His Glory – and they begat the book of Common Worship. And, as these have developed, so has the number of available choices of liturgy. We have moved from one Prayer of Consecration to four, and then to eight different variations. While the motives for these changes have been worthy and concerned the outcome has been that one can no longer talk about a single Book of Common Prayer: in their attempts to answer the criticisms of those who lament the demise of the old liturgies the new versions have been rather self-consciously wordy. The language of the Alternative Service Book, while rather banal on occasion, does have the advantage of speaking to the more down to earth ethos of the much wider constituency to which the Church aspires to minister.

I just wonder whether all this was not at the back of Jesus's mind when he held up the bread and broke it, saying, 'This is my body...'

Chapter 6

THE BREAD OF LIFE

One of the longest running debates about Jesus is that which considers the extent to which he was aware that he would be killed (and whether he was completely at the mercy of the Jewish council) or whether he manipulated the Passover occasion in order to stage a showdown with the forces of organized and particular religion.

Certainly the Passover supper – which he and his disciples shared – was marked by a sense of foreboding (as the secrecy of its location suggest) and no other occasion would have been so appropriate as a link between God's liberation of the Hebrews through the Plagues of Egypt and the Crossing of the Red Sea and the liberation of all humanity from the slavery of the law.

On that Passover evening Jesus declared in the simplest and most profound drama the core of what his life was all about. He took the basic foods of even the poorest of people – bread and wine – and symbolically associated them with God's saving purpose: remaking humans in his image; sharers in his Creation. He broke the bread and said, 'This is my body.' He passed the cup and said, 'This is my blood.' And to the Jews, for whom sacrifice was the only way of appeasing God, he offered them a new sacrifice – the sacrifice of his life – demanded by those who saw in him as a threat to the tidy interpretation and administration of the Torah, but also required as the only way of demonstrating that nothing – not even death – could prevent love from breaking through. And he said, 'Do this to remember me.'

And ever since that time either the Lord's Supper, the Eucharist or the Mass has been the central rite in the Christian Church. However, during the time since the Reformation the Bible and preaching have to some extent downgraded the importance of the sacrament, but there has been a revival in the last century (in the Church of England and in the Church of Rome) and this has stimulated much of the revision of the liturgy. Perhaps most importantly it is responsible for changing the emphasis of the liturgy from a private communion with God to a feast in which the gathering together to receive the broken bread and the wine makes Christ present in those elements. Herein is another profound truth: the fact that we take the body and blood of Christ right into our very being as nourishment means that we are renewed by the living body of Jesus himself. So we are set free from the old struggle of trying to copy Jesus, of following his instructions, and we are remade in the image of God and regenerated by his spirit of love for the whole world. Where Jesus is way ahead of us we struggle to keep up with him, which means we are no better off than we were under the law: where Jesus is in us we are transformed into his image – the image of God himself.

So we all come together in our room and we meet round a table for our fellowship meal, and we are aware of a great sense of oneness in Christ as we hold up our hands to receive the sacrament…except that the reality is often quite different. The personal relationship with God which has been the hallmark of the Reformed tradition means that for most communicants their approach to the altar is characterized more by feelings of private and personal communion with God and at that moment we are oblivious of the rest of the world, including our fellow church members.

Much the same feeling tends to surface when we say what is known as the Peace and shake hands with our neighbours in the pews. Apart from being rather un-English to be so pally in church, there is always the danger of the obvious intimacy of some becoming a barrier to newer and less outgoing worshippers. One of the great advantages of the more traditional church buildings is that they enable the hesitant to be drawn gently into the fellowship without being subjected to the claustrophobic bedlam which characterizes some places.

Yet it is desperately important that we move away from the purely individual approach to our communion. One way of solving the Peace problem in a conventional church building might be for the priest to come down into the middle of the congregation and ask them all to face whichever of the two sexes he or she represents. Then the introduction can be said, making sure that you face every one at some point, the main result of this being that the congregation have to face one another.

Nevertheless, we have to face the fact that formalization of worship is inevitable and necessary to enable the greater number of people of varying traditions and sensibilities to comfortably worship together. There is a greater need for that in the 21st century than there is for bigger churches and larger congregations.

The other great advantage of the Communion is that the depth of meaning and the simplicity and economy of the drama communicate to a much wider constituency than worship which relies solely on the spoken word – and which can only appeal to a relatively narrow range of culture, age and intellect. And if that also means that this encourages a sense of the mystical, then we shall be that much nearer to a better appreciation of God.

But of course the drama needs a stage and, however prosaic and matter-of-fact this modern age has become we cannot deny that God speaks to us through all the senses. As we have already noted, much of the appeal of the Communion service is that it is visual – but we also acknowledge that the drama needs a stage. So the setting – whether it be a large church, a domestic or church room used for an informal Mass or a niche set aside for private prayer with a table and one or two kneelers – all must be furnished and arranged to be compatible with our notion and awareness of the living God. So far as the Church is concerned most buildings will have a lot to say about God and his place in the world and the community. Order, harmony and beauty typify so many of our church buildings in this country.

However, the development of new theological insights is often obstructed by the design and the furnishings of a different age. The separation of sanctuary and congregation – often emphasized by the Victorian addition of a rood screen – is a valid if incomplete expression of our relationship with God, but it can make too much of a separation in an age which understands the celebration of the Mass as something that the priest and the congregation engage in together. However, if the attempts to change the emphasis are too draconian the result can speak more of disintegration than the new emphasis intended. It may be just as appropriate for a church to forego a particular reordering in order to avoid just such a clash. It isn't just a matter of offending the older and more reactionary members of the congregation; it may also be a denial of the faith journey of which the community is a part and the eternal truths that the buildings and their furnishings represent. On the other hand, the protection of some of the grotesque private family memorials – which occupy a position of eminence in so many old churches – represent the less acceptable face of patronage, and as places of worship are ill-served by preservation orders and the obstructive legal challenges of non-attending parishioners.

As with architecture and design, so with music. The Anglican and the Methodist churches of Britain have a tradition of hymnody which is second to none, and many of their hymns have become classics whose place is assured in worship for years to come. 'Teach me my God and King' by George Herbert and Samuel Crossman's 'My song is love unknown' are two of the best known and loved. Many others are much too dated – such as the verse in 'All things bright and beautiful':

> 'The rich man in his castle,
> The poor man at his gate,
> God made them high and lowly
> And ordered their estate.'

However, many that were written in Victorian times represent some of the least attractive tunes and sentiments and no tears need be shed at their demise.

In between we are often presented with a dilemma in that words which on their own are inspiring lose their impact when coupled with music which is inferior or simply inappropriate – and vice versa. What is to be deplored are the attempts to put Christian words to tunes in the modern pop idiom with the result that the style of the music is totally incompatible with the sentiments of the words. Yet I cannot remember anything more appropriate and moving musically than a piano piece of modern jazz by Thelonius Monk played at the end of a funeral service.

Of course there need to be hymns and songs whose musical language is immediately accessible to the ear, but that does not mean that any old popular tune will do. For whatever reason, there has been too much music in which the words and the music simply contradict each other. Mostly churches in this country seem to have gone one way or the other, either succumbing to the tyranny of a real organist, 'If you introduce the modern service (or an electronic organ) you will have to find another organist', or 'the young people have no time for boring old hymns, so we will use the modern worship songs'. As someone once said, 'You don't have to like music by Graham Kendrick to be a Christian.'

Much of what can be presented musically in worship is dependent upon the availability of musical skills in the individual church. In many places, sadly, the vocal and choral tradition of the Church has given way to the instrumental, so that the average age of choirs increases, and those who reach real competence in their instruments are often at the awkward age and have other things to do with their Sunday mornings. Perhaps one of the developments which has been most appropriate to this age of musical transition has been the material produced under the auspices of the Roman Catholic Church by musicians such as Christopher Walker, Paul Inwood, Bernadette Farrell and others. They have produced accessible music – vocal and instrumental – which recognizes the availability of a few good musicians along with a larger number of willing, though hitherto unappreciated voices.

Sadly, many churches – especially the smaller and less well-endowed – can boast neither organist nor competent keyboard player in their fellowship. Fortunately we now have sound systems – which use recorded banks of hymns and other accompaniments – and which only need to be switched on and the tunes preselected to enable the leader to set each one going. When we saw these once at one of the Christian resources exhibitions I took a particular liking to one in which the operator could not only choose the verses of the hymn but also the key and the tempo. But perhaps that puts too much power in the hands of one person.

Another opportunity which recorded music presents is the playing of the tapes and discs of well-known sacred music as part of a meditation. Opportunities of this sort present themselves on such occasions as All Souls, at a time of national or international disaster such as the death of Princess Diana, the tragedy in New York in 2001 or to accompany the Good Friday Stations of the Cross.

It is difficult, however, to know just how far along this road to go for the more that we relay second-hand elements into our worship the less we take an active part. Worship is after all what we do and there are limits to being able to be fully and personally involved in things we receive from outside ourselves.

Then there is the vexed question of organ playing. As national church attendance has dwindled fewer and fewer people learn this instrument: competent pianists are often intimidated by an idiosyncratic organ or one which has too few stops or a heavy action and, sadly, there is a lot of snobbery which will not countenance the purchase of a much cheaper electronic instrument. But modern instruments now bear no resemblance to the old-time cinema organ, and they have facilities which go a long way towards enabling any competent keyboard player to become reasonably proficient on their instrument.

Not long ago one church persuaded an organist on the international recital circuit to be principal artiste in a Gospel of Music and Light concert to celebrate the installation of the new electronic organ along with new computerized lighting, which had varying scenes to capture different moods of worship. When asked what he thought of the organ he said, 'It's very good for plastic – but it's 24-carat plastic.'

And of course lighting is an essential tool of worship. There is so much allusion to light and dark in the Bible that it is an essential part of this consideration. Although the modern systems are expensive the effects can transform a church and make the very best of its features.

When I was a teacher of Religious Studies we used to begin the 11- to 12-year-old youngsters' course with a survey of local churches on a map, with information and pictures which they gathered themselves. Then we used to take them into the local parish church and let them explore it. Several of them had never set foot in a church before but perhaps the thing that caught their attention more than any other was the banks of votive candles at the foot of the statues of Mary and the painting of Jesus. As they lit their candles for their Granny or their sick relation maybe the tiny flame – dwarfed by the subdued light in the big church – caught the mood of their little prayer making an impact in this huge and sometimes threatening world. They were certainly not fooling about.

I said earlier that the Communion service enabled everyone – no matter how diverse – to come together to make Christ present in the fellowship, and particularly this applies to children.

In these days of universal wealth in the fortunate west, what a wonderful resource for worship we can have with so much technology at our disposal. It was therefore quite salutary for me to move to the country into a little church which had none of the modern aids that I have described. Just a Book of Common Prayer and a hymn book. I suppose that all we really need is a loaf of bread, a bottle of wine and a Bible – but more than all these we need people.

Chapter 7

LIVING WATER

Let us go back to the Samaritan woman at the well.

> *Jesus said to her, 'Will you give me a drink?' The Samaritan woman said to him, 'You are a Jew and I am a Samaritan woman. How can you ask me for a drink?'*
>
> *Jesus answered her, 'If you knew the gift of God – and who it is who asks you for a drink – you would have asked him and he would have given you living water.'*
>
> *'Sir,' the woman said, 'You have nothing to draw with and the well is deep. Where can you get this living water? Are you greater than our father Jacob – who gave us the well and drank from it himself – as did also his sons and his flocks and herds?'*
>
> *Jesus answered, 'Everyone who drinks this water will be thirsty again, but whoever drinks the water I give him will never thirst. Indeed, the water I give him will become in him a spring of water welling up to eternal life.'*

The theme of water runs right through the Old and New Testaments and this is hardly surprising, since the lands involved experience both desert and flood conditions as well as storms and scorching heat. So water by turns became a threat and a disaster – and an essential of life – be it for cleaning or drinking.

We have already touched on the seeming incongruity of Jesus being baptized by John, but we also remember that John made the distinction between his own baptism by water and Jesus's baptism by the Holy Spirit and with fire.

Human beings' perceptions of their own wrongdoings produce very differing reactions. Where the way of life is held up as a series of dos and don'ts we measure ourselves against the norm and react according to our sense of success or failure. Where this process has started in youth and a draconian set of rules has been laid down we find religious groups and psychiatric units trying to handle the casualties weighed down – often indeed nearly destroyed – by their sense of guilt. It is the easiest thing in the world to use guilt in the religious context. It is the hardest thing to reverse its devastating effects. This had a lot to do with the Gospels' accounts of Jesus's opposition to the Pharisees.

When we meet the Samaritan woman at the well we notice a lack of burden – indeed a great sense of joy. Jesus has somehow become aware of her past, one that might these days qualify for a spicy article in a tabloid newspaper. But her, 'Come and see a man who told me everything that I ever did,' has a ring of relief and a sense of joy that someone could be so concerned to know her that well.

The effect that an encounter with Jesus had on people meant that they did not feel that there were any barriers between them and him. Yet beside him they became aware of just how far short they were of what they could become. Here there is a penitence that is not overburdened with guilt but charged with hope. And this was the necessary prelude to being baptized with the Holy Spirit and with fire – receiving the gift of love and thereby being assured of our presence with God at judgement.

The language of penitence and confession has in the

past been too heavily loaded with expressions of guilt, and recent theological fashion has tended to gloss over the human characteristic of sin – or putting oneself at the centre of the universe. But the constant awareness that we fall so far short of the love displayed by Jesus must make us want to come to him, knowing that he will pick us up and feed us with his spirit. He does not want us to wallow in our misdoings but he does want us to acknowledge our sins and to ask forgiveness for them – not only from God but also from those we have wronged. But he then wants us to look forward, knowing that he has forgiven us. Asking forgiveness of other humans and apologizing for our wrongdoing is one of the hardest things we are called upon to do, and it often seems that the more high profile we are in our faith the harder we find it.

Walking with a sense of penitence, therefore, is not a negative attitude. On the contrary, it opens us up to being able to receive Jesus and be indwelt by Him. That is why so many Christians appreciate the presence of water available to them either in the font near the entrance to the Church, or in a small stoup if the font is protected by a cover. By dipping the fingers in, with or without making the sign of the Cross, we put ourselves once again in the situation where Jesus can invite us to receive him in the spirit.

It is quite a problem that the popular perception of baptism is so far removed from its real meaning. When parents apply to have their children – not always babies – baptized, their reason is usually expressed in terms of a 'blessing' or 'doing the right thing'. It is also tied up with a family celebration whose urgency is determined by the relative size of the baby concerned and the christening garment to be worn.

Let's eavesdrop on a typical family – a two-year-old arrives at her grandparents' house, goes straight to the toy box and proceeds to get everything out and spread it all over the floor until there is not a spare inch that hasn't got a tiger, a dinosaur, a piece of monster puzzle or a sheet with stickers all over it. Now there is the raw material for a discussion in which there is a debate between parents and grandparents on whether a two-year-old can understand the sense of getting only one toy out at a time, and also whether it is wise to make an issue out of something or to distract the child's attention to avoid it.

Forty years ago one didn't ask questions like that. We all knew the answers to such a situation and basically agreed on them. And so in both school and home there was a consensus that parental and school authority were accepted because everyone was more or less agreed that both the institutions and the rules were common to all.

In the years that have succeeded that time there has been a vast change and now there seem to be few accepted norms and even fewer accepted authorities. As each psychological fashion has succeeded the previous one we have changed our approach and now we are no longer sure about anything – and we are quite sure that whatever we do we will damage our children irreparably, especially if we don't allow them to express themselves.

So what are young people being told in schools? Where I was told, 'This is right and do it because I say so', more recent generations are told, 'Here are the options – now you choose. These are the ways you might react. It's right if it is right for you. There is no absolute right and wrong; it depends on the situation. You choose between ethical egoism, situation ethics or utilitarianism.

But – and here is a huge great but – at the same time it is becoming more and more clear that the universe is a system in which every tiniest part is linked to another and any change in one small aspect has a knock-on effect into the rest of the system. It is a cliché that if trees in the Brazilian rainforest are cut down then carbon dioxide builds up and heat accumulates in the atmosphere; that combustion of fossil fuels destroys the ozone layer and harmful rays of sunlight penetrate into the earth's atmosphere; that if we cut down trees in an area of forest then we may cause floods which threaten communities lower down the valley; that if you go to war with a country and make humiliating demands of reparation it is not too surprising if they vote in a government such as Hitler's to restore their national self-esteem.

To put it in a nutshell we are agreed that we live in a complex world of interrelationships but at the same time we are saying fundamentally that it's each person for himself. Each person decides what is right by his own lights – from his or her own perspective.

I have stated it fairly crudely to emphasize that this is a fundamental contradiction.

So, really, there is only one alternative. That if there is to be harmony in this world it has got to be as a result of everything being focused through one purpose, one direction, one being whose whole drive is towards harmony and integration: the perfection, if you like, of the universe. And that is what we mean by God.

So there is a simple choice, and that is between self-rule (individualism) or God. And we know, of course, exactly what happens when self-rule wins. Someone will fight their way to the top and attempt to control everyone else. But the trouble with the other alternative is that God doesn't reveal himself sufficiently clearly. So, in order to be able to get our minds around God, we were given Jesus.

And when we bring our children to baptism we are saying this – that we realize all human beings have a natural tendency to put themselves at the centre of the universe, and that all human beings have to consciously reject that: repent and sign on to the truth that we have to put the God whom we know in Jesus at the centre of our universe if we are to 'play our part in bringing life to the world.' And when we bring our children to baptism we are saying that only by immersing them in the whole culture of putting God at the centre of our lives will they be brought to do the same.

And we certainly can't expect our children to do more than we are prepared to do ourselves.

In one of the baptisms in our church we filled the font with water from a wash jug and a watering can because we wanted to show that the water of baptism represents our washing away of our sins (the wash jug) and the new life (the watering can) that we have when we put Jesus at the centre of our universe. But I left out perhaps the most important piece of symbolism. The whole essence of what Jesus was all about was about drowning – to the life of putting ourselves first, drowning the self, submerging our selfish desires and putting the needs of others right up there with our own. From our point of view it means an actual sacrifice for the needs of others, and actually demands that in certain cases. In practice it usually means that we become just a bit more aware of and are concerned for others.

But at the same time we have to recognize that because human beings by nature do the opposite of this, then we have to get involved in the community of those who want to put God first. We realize that we need to mix with others of the same mind, that we need to be kept in touch with the life, the ministry and the teaching of Jesus, that we need to allow the Holy Spirit to make the same sort of transformation in our lives as he did in those of the disciples when they met together in that room at Pentecost.

Now it's one thing to talk about a community whose hallmark is self-sacrifice and quite another to be recognized as that sort of community. Because we are human we talk a better community than we act, so to speak, and therein perhaps lies the problem with the Church. It's a community of human beings – and human beings are weak and have failings – and Christians in that sense are no different, except for this: as the Church we are, whether we like it or not, the body of Christ – a community of people who have committed themselves to letting God be the lord of our lives. And Jesus Christ, through whom we know God, has already won the victory over the sin of human beings on the Cross.

So what we are saying is that humans by nature put themselves in the centre of the universe, get it wrong, miss the mark, sin (to use religious jargon) but – by acknowledging God as the only being who can integrate all the parts of the universe – we can be set free to play the part that we were designed for. By giving up our self-rule and submitting ourselves to God and his law then – and only then – can the world become a harmonious whole.

And we certainly can't expect our children to do more than we are prepared to do ourselves.

Now we think it is very important that families who want a baptism should have the opportunity of understanding what it is all about and that they should realize what they are saying and promising to do. Very few are put off by this yet one can't help feeling – and experience bears this out – that few are going to reappear in church of their own accord. Nevertheless, as Christians in a community we should feel that ideally we have a responsibility to bring everyone into the Church and if we are filled with God's Spirit and praying trustfully, we symbolize that in offering baptism.

Infant baptism is a bit like taking an old-fashioned film photograph. We arrange the picture in the viewfinder, we press the shutter and – bingo – we have the picture – yet we don't, for everyone realizes that before that happens the film has to be developed and printed. If the parents, the godparents and the Church all play their part then what might have been a meaningless ceremony becomes a reality and in God's good time the baptized take their place in the company of saints. If the godparents lose touch with their godchild a great opportunity is lost. If the parents fail to keep their part of the bargain the child's spiritual nurture is set back. But if the Church does not do anything to make the sacrament more than just a hollow ceremony, then that child has really been let down – the roll of film remains in the camera, with the possibility that the captured image never sees the light of day. For the Church has particular responsibility for ensuring that it speaks of our love of God, the greatness of God, and that we don't just leave things to other people. And those who bring their children to baptism have a responsibility for their children's future.

How do we measure responsibility? Well, I think it has something to do with the depth and the breadth of what we consider we are or should be involved in. And most people these days are pretty responsible, in their job and in the home. It is reasonable, therefore, to think that we take our responsibilities for our children no less seriously and extensively and that we also take responsibility for the wider community in which the children will grow (and we will look to the future, as well). And that's why I believe that the really deeply-thinking person will be more likely to say 'Yes' to God than 'Yes' to self-rule. It is more in tune with the world which we are beginning to understand.

So, put quite simply – in what I would say were fairly critical times – we are faced with the choice for ourselves and for our children of putting God or Self first. In human terms putting God first is well-nigh impossible but we are invited into a community – the Church – which, weak and human as it is, has been promised victory over our weakness.

And of course there are more and more people who do not find faith until years later, and it warms the heart at Confirmations to see people of all ages coming to be baptized publicly and receiving the Holy Spirit in Confirmation. For some of them it will be in response to a dramatic conversion experience, for others a slow realization that they have (so to speak) crossed the Rubicon, and while for many years the divide between Catholic and Reformed traditions has been profound and divisive on this issue there has been much more understanding and flexibility in recent years.

And each time that we are present at a baptism we are given the opportunity to re-identify with those who know how easily, even as Christians, we put ourselves at the centre of the universe. How very tempted we are, time and again, to say with the Pharisee, 'I thank you, Lord, that I am not as others are. I am a regular churchgoer, I give ten per cent of my disposable income to charity and I feel I have a responsibility to live an honest and pure life as a witness in these amoral times.' So we are given the chance to join in as we declare our commitment to God in Christ and we pray for and welcome those who have been baptized – aware that our prayers and our witness are crucial in the new Christian's spiritual journey – and we have another opportunity to say with the publican, 'Lord, have mercy on me, a sinner.'

How can we not mean that when we put ourselves beside Jesus, but at the same time our confidence in his acceptance of us as we are means that our guilt need never drag us down for we rely on his promise to live his life in and through us – and be his love for the world – and if we trust in this, then at the least we have hope and our realised hope gradually builds our faith.

And I don't think we have realised how much we, as a global community, have departed from the baptismal culture. And this is particularly the case in our own national life.

We are soaked now in a culture of blame, where issues are discussed and evaluated in terms of right and wrong. So we are too easily obsessed by the search for the right or correct approach to any particular issue. Having identified what we conceive to be the right action or concept, either through prayer or our understanding of the Bible's teaching, our conscience tells us that we are in the right and we pursue its execution with all the fervour of moral superiority. So those who do not agree with us are wrong and immediately we have thrown up this barrier. And it is just this sort of approach that can eventually leads to issues being polarized, even to the length of breaking our ties with fellow Christians.

But surely St Paul has dealt with this problem when he says, 'Now we see through a glass darkly but then, (i.e. in heaven) face to face.' All have sinned and fallen short of the glory of God. So for Christians it is not on to trumpet our position and excoriate those who oppose us. Come let us reason together – and do so keeping in mind that we only have a limited view (we say) – of all the options this one seems to be the least tarnished. Let us sit down and work through our differences, each coming a bit nearer to a consensus. In this way we broaden our view and keep the relationship.

But how can we prevent the sort of conflict we have over issues which tear the Church and churches apart? I would suggest that where the emphasis lies solely on scripture, creeds and doctrines it is very difficult to prevent them becoming like a sort of latter-day set of Commandments, and Jesus reminds us that every Commandment has to be interpreted in the light of our loving God, and loving our neighbours as ourselves, which means that we must keep the relationship by not putting ourselves on a morally higher plain than the neighbour. That is where we must emphasize the confession but also move on to receiving the Holy Spirit in the bread and wine.

Chapter 8

PRAYER

I like the story of the young American soldier who, having finished his training, was drafted to an active unit. He was a devout Christian and made a habit of kneeling down each evening in prayer. He was teased for this, not least by the sergeant, who never missed an opportunity to ridicule his faith. The time came when the unit was drafted to the front line and the platoon found itself suddenly under heavy shell-fire. As they had been trained to do the men quickly dug themselves into foxholes to afford some sort of protection. In the ensuing bombardment the young soldier was aware of being joined in a hurry by another soldier who, as the shelling became more intense, was heard to pray fervently to God for protection. In a lull in the bombardment the soldier took the opportunity to look at his neighbour, only to discover – to his astonishment – that it was the sergeant. 'But, Sergeant,' he said, 'I thought you were an atheist.' To which the Sergeant replied, 'Son, there are no atheists in foxholes.'

Among the family mementos which I treasure is a rosary. It was given to one of my uncles – a graduate of Birmingham School of Art – by a French peasant, not long before he was killed on the first day of the Battle of the Somme in 1916. It was obviously a cheap one, for the design is very simple and the links have rusted. Coming from a Unitarian background

– with an understanding of faith which my Grandfather described as 'reverent agnosticism' –it is likely that he did not fully appreciate the rosary as an aid to prayer, yet I feel sure that it would have been one of the things that comforted him as he prepared for action and I have a sneaking suspicion that his artistic sensibilities might have given him an appreciation of its symbolic relevance.

Praying is one of the things that comes most naturally to humans and time and time again even the most self-sufficient of people find themselves in the situation where they feel compelled to pray. The sceptic might say that this does not mean that there is a God or that if there is he hears – let alone answers – our prayers. But if Jesus felt the need to pray then how much more likely are we to need that, too?

There can be very few people who have not been reduced to shouting for help – first, obviously, from their fellow humans – but then, when there is no one else, to call out to someone or something out there (quite likely in sheer desperation as much as in any expectation of an answer). Of course, it is too easy to say that this is just wishful thinking, but if we are honest we have to concede that this very pervasive attitude is shared by too many to dismiss it as empty. So we have to look at the other alternative.

The first time I was conscious of prayer in my own life was as a student in Burgos Cathedral in Castile, and I went into one of the small chapels and felt a compulsion to kneel down at the altar rail but it certainly did not lead me to take my obligatory church or chapel attendance any more seriously.

So nothing happened really until I was thrown in at the deep end when I went to stay for the first time with my girl-friend at her vicarage home. Suddenly after breakfast I found myself involved in family prayers – as a passive witness – and overcome with embarrassment. This was a form of prayer which I had never experienced before and its intimacy and informality were so far removed from the Book of Common Prayer and the more formal style of school prayers that I felt uncomfortable. But what it did do was to make me realize that prayer is intimate and personal as well as formal and corporate. A year later I made a public commitment of faith.

As we read more spiritual guide books so we learn about different forms of prayer, silence, meditation, prayer meetings, mantras, collects, the rosary and so on. We also learn that there are different places for prayer – in church services, in chapels, in cathedrals, in religious houses but also anywhere else: in the car, in the bathroom, walking along the road, on top of a mountain and – believe it or not – on the rugby field. Perhaps one of the most difficult situations for prayer, however, is in a church or cathedral or chapel, as a member of a choir.

But we all struggle with prayer, in one way or another and, for that reason, while we feel nothing but admiration for those who clearly are – or whose reputations go before them as a man or woman of prayer – there is also a sense of frustration in having their example held up before us, as if to say, 'That is your target – see how near you can get to it.'

And if we are to pray we want to know that what we are doing is worthwhile and effective. Does prayer work? we ask ourselves. If I pray for others will my prayers be answered? Jesus said, 'If two of you shall agree on anything that you ask in my name I will grant it.' So we get together and pray that Sam's tumour might be healed – or that so-and-so will be appointed to a parish, or that our son might not marry the girl whom he is living with (or for that matter live with the girl whom he might marry). If our prayer is granted we are delighted and may even remember to thank God for it – but if it is not we are given the following explanations: that we had insufficient faith; that God wanted to teach us a lesson; that he said 'no,' or 'wait' instead of 'yes'; that we had not prayed 'in the name of Jesus', that he had granted our prayer but not in the way we expected – and, particularly – that so-and-so has been healed, but spiritually. With these sort of arguments it is impossible to lose a debate on the effectiveness of prayer.

But while all this might be going on in our minds we come up against a real crisis and we simply implore God to hear us and to heal, to change, to provide and to save. And despite our mental reservations we feel absolutely authentic in our prayer; that we have a heavenly father – Abba, who hears our prayer, that we trust him, and we acknowledge our inability to deal with the issue on our own.

And there is no conflict between these apparent contradictions. It is a situation which many people share – in fact I would hazard a guess that it applies to the majority. Here is another situation where Paul's comment about 'seeing in a glass darkly' is so apt. Our reason and our faith can take us only so far in our knowledge and understanding of prayer – it is when they both seem to desert us that we get to our knees. And we come to terms with it particularly when we realize that most of us have been praying in the wrong direction. We start off with our own agenda and set it out before God. 'This is the situation, God – and here is the solution – so please get on with it (if you don't mind and – oh, yes, "In the name of Jesus" – and "where two or three are gathered together").'

And eventually, when this doesn't seem to work, or we have been at it for a long time, we stop – and – well, we start to listen.

And yes, the pattern of our prayer is there before us in the life of Jesus. And one of the things that seems to typify his prayer is that he regularly withdrew from his friends and from all the people who wanted to see and hear him, and went off to a lonely place.

'One of those days Jesus went out to a mountainside to pray, and spent the night praying to God.'
'After he had dismissed them he went up on a mountainside by himself to pray. When evening came, he was there alone...'

Right at the beginning – after his baptism – he went to the wilderness and waited on God and fought this battle within himself as to how he was going to win people's hearts. Yes, he fought temptation, but so much prayer is a struggle between what we want and what God wants. And at some point we discover that we have moved from asking for or demanding this or that to listening to what God wants.

Perhaps the greatest example that Jesus gives us is his struggle in Gethsemane:

Going a little farther, he fell to the ground and prayed that if possible the hour might pass from him. 'Abba, Father,' he said, 'Everything is possible for you. Take this cup from me... and then, because he has spent all night in prayer, much later... 'Yet not what I will, but what you will.'

Then he returned to his disciples and found them sleeping. 'Simon,' he said to Peter, 'Are you asleep? Could you not keep watch for one hour? Watch and pray so that you will not fall into temptation. The spirit is willing, but the body is weak.' Once more he went away and prayed the same thing. When he came back he again found them sleeping, because their eyes were heavy. They did not know what to say to him.

'Again, I tell you that if two of you on earth agree about anything you ask for, it will be done for you by my Father in heaven. For where two or three come together in my name, there am I with them.'

Some people prefer to pray together, often in impromptu style – with no direction other than perhaps when there is a pressing need over which the Church is concerned – or as a means to starting and ending the meeting. For many churches this is the most important type of prayer.

But it is not for everyone and those who shy away from it need to feel that their sensibilities are not dismissed lightly and their particular style may be as authentic and genuine as anyone else's. Jesus must have had a reason for saying,

> *'But when you pray, go into your room, close the door and pray to your Father, who is unseen. Then your Father, who sees what is done in secret, will reward you. And when you pray do not keep on babbling like pagans, for they think they will be heard because of their many words. Do not be like them, for your Father knows what you need before you ask him.'*

But I can also hear the response of so many people: 'Where am I going to find the time to be on my own – for ten minutes, let alone an hour?' This is from the mother of two under-fives, whose father doesn't get home until eight if he's lucky: the elder has already started at primary school, while the younger goes to a playgroup three mornings a week. Being a qualified accountant she is using that freedom to keep her hand in and has taken on a few private clients – with their huge mortgage she needs to…from the teacher who heads a science department in a large comprehensive school… faced with a mountain of course work to moderate, compounded by the problems of an inexperienced junior teacher, all of whose course work he has had to re-mark himself. He leaves the house at 6.30am so that he can have an hour or so before the pupils and his colleagues arrive because the school has an impending

OFSTED inspection...from the vicar who convenes a meeting at 7.30 am so that the Church primary school board of governors can all be present at a crucial meeting, and then drives to a diocesan subcommittee 20 miles away.

Yes, sad to say, even the Church is caught up in the rush. And, while all the books of pastoral guidance stress the need for prayer, I wonder just how very busy their authors turn out to be. This particular one cannot avoid the accusation, and has to plead guilty as charged.

And it is not that we haven't been reminded. To my consternation – as a modern vicar – I once found myself not only carless but bikeless. I had to do something that is only done by young people in sports kit, and childfree couples in hiking kit – that is, to walk. And because instead of five minutes I took 15, I found myself actually thinking and reflecting. Yet at that point I did not even possess a mobile phone, and while I had a computer I only used it as a word processor and a filing system. Just imagine Archimedes with a cordless or mobile phone within arm's reach of the bath, or Newton absorbed in a problem on his laptop, with the apples falling around him.

In response to this situation there has been a great increase in interest in religious retreats. Indeed we ought properly to widen this description to include those of no religion who realize the need to step out of the maelstrom; to take stock of their lives in a place set aside for reflection and silent meditation. This has become a major part of the ministry of the religious houses and can be of great value. The perception of life in a religious community and the anticipation of total silence for even 24 hours can be very daunting, but there are few who don't surprise themselves by coming away tremendously refreshed and recommending it to their friends. The retreats vary a lot – some leave you entirely to yourself, others might have a series of talks and a counsellor to listen to those who need guidance. Others again may involve you more completely in the life of the community. What usually happens is that one's encounters with the monastic life mean that you meet a group of Christians who are more down to earth than those escaping from the real world.

And one of the legacies which these religious communities have left us is the Daily Office, which one might call the secular version of the series of prayers which punctuate the daily life of the community. The basic outline is confession, Psalms and spiritual songs, scripture readings, further canticles or Psalm-like songs and prayers. There is a shorter version for the less ambitious or more realistic. But the essence of these is that they establish a pattern which becomes part of a routine and this, far from becoming meaningless, often surprises us by showing us something new after years of use. And, because they become ingrained, they are a real port in the storms which periodically beat down upon us.

So when Advent and Lent come round each year we are, so to speak, given a chance to start all over again in our life of prayer. We make a special effort to set aside a time, and we go to our corner at home, in the conservatory, at our prayer desk, or in the Lady Chapel, or wherever and come before God and just, well... be ourselves before him. To start with it is all us: we bring with us the thing which is on our mind, the people whom we are concerned about both positively and negatively. We are completely honest about what we feel, what we fear, what we want and we lay it all before God. Frequently we have no words to express our needs so we resort to repeating over and over again, 'Lord, have mercy, Lord, have mercy.' We may even want to shout at God, to make him listen. We turn to scripture, particularly the Psalms and the Gospels and then turn back to our thoughts – and imperceptibly we change. Our racing anxieties slow down, we become less important, and we find ourselves saying, 'Lord, not our will but yours be done.'

And so often what happens is that we experience nothing – and then looking back we realize that things have changed; that we have changed. So much of spiritual growth seems to be experienced retrospectively. And with that experience we find our prayer being narrowed down to asking God to take us into his mind – that his will may be done – and filling us with that spirit of love and inclusiveness which we see in Jesus and that we feel that we can never achieve, except by his grace.

Yet prayer is so much more than all this. We used to holiday in south Worcestershire and it was often at the time of the Three Choirs Festival when Worcester, Gloucester and Hereford cathedrals took it in turn to host some marvellous choral singing. To sit in the cheap seats in Gloucester was no hardship because the acoustic enabled one to hear perfectly in any seat, with the advantage that since the orchestra was invisible the architecture took over and one was lost to the normal world outside as the forms of the building, Newman's poetry and Elgar's music spoke of a spiritual dimension that too often escapes us. Gerontius, in his dream, sings:

> I went to sleep and now I am refreshed.
> A strange refreshment: for I feel in me
> An inexpressive lightness, and a sense
> Of freedom, as I were at length myself,
> And ne'er had been before. How still it is!
> I hear no more the busy beat of time,
> No, nor my fluttering breath, nor struggling pulse;
> Nor does one moment differ from the next.

But any solitary walk provides the context in which we can meet God – and that will depend on the sort of relationship we have with him. For the extent to which he gets hold of us is not up to us, it is up to God ,and when he does there is not much you can do about it. And more than anything else God makes you think honestly – which, come to think of it, is largely what it's all about.

Chapter 9

MAKING CONNECTIONS

I can't really imagine what my life would have been like if I had not had my encounter with Jesus of Nazareth nearly 40 years ago. I wonder what its focus would have been, what my ambitions would have been and how my life would have been different.

In the early years I found great encouragement to talk about my faith with others who were like-minded, and at an early stage we became members of a very lively church which had only been going for four years and which worshipped in a converted medieval tithe barn. This church had a very outgoing approach to faith and was fortunate in that it was not weighed down by the dead hand of excessive tradition and civic flummery. It was particularly successful in making contact with the young families moving into the mushrooming estates of the 1960s and 1970s, and soon began to outgrow its accommodation. So two main Sunday morning services were held and numerous groups met in the week for Bible study and other topics relevant to the nurture and sharing of faith. As a result the Church developed a very close sense of fellowship and commitment which enabled it to initiate and support not only its own impressive growth but other Christian ministries both locally, nationally and especially in the foreign mission field.

As I have already mentioned I became involved in Bible

studies for boys in the schools I taught in which had connections with national societies for the evangelism of young
people, and we often had visits from their representative
youth workers. The focus of their work was the camps organized for secondary school children, which provided wonderfully professional activity holidays with a time each day for a
sequential presentation of the Christian faith in a style which
was particularly accessible to the age groups concerned.

But in both the above cases, and among my growing
number of friends who came through them, I found that there
was a great distinction drawn between those who were real
Christians and those who were described as nominal. To start
with I took this on board and found that it began to make me
look on those around me and wonder, or decide, into which of
these categories they fell.

The problem was that too many of us who presumed to
evaluate others' faith were armed with precious little knowledge, experience or humility. At worst a person's spiritual-
ity was judged by whether they smoked or drank alcohol or
swore, and at best by their attendance at church.

Well, that said, rugby players were damned several times
over – but you can't spend half the Saturdays of the year with
many of the same people without them becoming enduring if not close friends – and the very suggestion that such
people would no longer count as friends was one of the things
that made me begin to feel uneasy and slightly at odds with
the expression of Christianity through which I had so far
journeyed.

Mercifully very few Christians seem take this line now
but there is still a great temptation to see the Christian faith
as a moral crusade, battling against an increasingly evil world
and one which has abandoned the moral truths of the previous
generations.

In one recent evangelistic campaign sponsored by the churches of a Home Counties town, the title of the series of talks around which the campaign was mounted was the Ten Commandments. The process of persuasion was conducted with all the skills of the market trader, including the humour, the gestures and the repartee. Yet the young man's obvious pride in being able to discomfit a supermarket checkout girl and, on another occasion, a teenage lad in the back row of a school assembly simply showed that his zeal ran far ahead of his understanding and compassion for young people.

This campaign was the climax of a three-year ecumenical project for the millennium. It cost £16,000, generated a huge amount of local coverage and consumed the energies of a large proportion of the church members of the community. Yet it was impossible to say whether it was an effective use of the church's members' time, energy and money. Those who were anxious to be able to declare the number of converts, i.e. non-churchgoers who were converted to the faith, could only point to an insignificant few – for most of those who attended were churchgoers already, and went along as supporters as much as to learn something new.

But this method of evangelism is generally considered to be out of date, and calls to mind the Billy Graham crusades of the 1950s onwards. These were national campaigns – mostly centred on the metropolises – and backed by a large supporting cast which made real efforts to connect those who had responded to the challenge of faith to their local church. Their commitment to keeping in touch with these converts – sometimes for many years – was admirable, but was too often emasculated by the failure of the local church to provide the support needed.

The most recent campaign, which has been going for eight years or so, took another tack. It was developed under the auspices of the Holy Trinity church in Brompton (Kensington) and was a course for Christian enquiry: it involved groups of enquirers whose gathering focused on a common meal and who, after a presentation of a faith topic, were encouraged to discuss it and share their thoughts. There is no specific call to faith but the climax of the course is a residential weekend in which participants are encouraged to have an experience of the Holy Spirit, towards which they are guided by the leaders setting up a session in which there is a heavy expectation of something going to happen. Those who have been to such gatherings have experienced various sensations from feeling warm, a great sense of elation – and even more extreme manifestations, which cause a few to cry out, to fall to the ground, or let out ecstatic cries.

However, there is a sizeable number of people for whom such a gathering poses a real threat and the ever-present danger – from enthusiastic but unwise counselling supporting attendants – makes the whole proceedings of the weekend fraught with a danger that is avoidable.

Part and parcel of the Alpha phenomenon is their advertising. Readers of the Church Times find that their regular copy is twice as thick as usual from time to time, and as often as not it will be because Alpha is advertising. And a great deal of that advertising is about the numbers who attend and the level of success achieved. And some of the statistics are truly staggering, representing – as they do – a tremendous degree of effort, of time and of commitment (though a closer examination of the graphs exhibited demonstrates a somewhat tendentious interpretation of the findings).

Yet there is a large number of people who feel uncomfortable with the whole culture of open evangelism and for whom this sort of expression of faith is not appropriate to them, yet who feel guilty for presuming to experience negative feelings when they come across such a successful phenomenon. As one of them I have had to look into my own conscience to try to ensure that my assessment is as fair and objective as possible.

I have made the point several times that one of the main things which registered with me –when I was seeking answers to questions of faith – was the impact that the character of Jesus had on me. The Alpha approach to Christ is fundamentally different. Here the writer sets out to prove the existence of God and the reasons for believing that Jesus is the Son of God. As each point is made so it is consolidated by anecdotal evidence and by appeals to logic and reason.

For many this simply doesn't work. My faith does not stem from being satisfied by reason, and intellectual certainty and faith deal with totally different parts of this human being. My faith is what makes me go on when sometimes my mind is saying something quite different. Yet at the same time my faith is eminently reasonable insofar as there are no philosophical no-go areas.

But it is perhaps the Alpha theology of the Cross which I think makes for such a negative view of God. The idea that God judges us is of course central to all Christian theology, but it also needs to be said that from the human point of view we judge ourselves in the light of our knowledge and love of Jesus. In the parable of the Prodigal Son it is not the father who makes the accusation but the son who realizes that he has sinned and who finds himself met more than half way by the open arms of the father. By suggesting that God is not satisfied until he has exacted payment for the wrongdoing (and this refers to payment by an innocent third party who is not only his Son but is one with the Father) is to preserve a theology which owes its construction to a very different age from the one we live in. In particular this ignores the important distinction between judgement of guilt and penalty.

Now although there are worrying signs that lex talionis – an eye for an eye and a tooth for a tooth – is becoming increasingly popular in the face of some highly publicized heinous crimes, nevertheless our penal system is still geared to the principles of reform, deterrent and protection of the community. We do not have the death penalty for capital offences and – particularly where young people are concerned – we are very conscious of the need to enable young offenders to put their misdeeds behind them and become responsible members of society.

Jesus's life revealed God in all the glory of his love for his Creation, a love which proved itself in him to be indestructible and which still proves the same through the actions of those who follow in his footsteps. If we see what Jesus did on the Cross in these very human terms, so we will realize that what was true for Jesus can be equally true for us. A cross – which is a transaction between God and his Son and therefore external to us – will never have the same impact and Jesus as well as God will still be out there with the result that, without meaning to, we will still be struggling to please God through our actions.

It is not too surprising, therefore, that when Alpha turns its attention to the Holy Spirit it misses the most crucial fact of all – and that is that God is love. Listen this time not to St Paul, who in spite of his conversion still retained much of his Pharisee heritage, but to St John:

> 'Dear friends, let us love one another – for love comes from God. Everyone who loves has been born of God and knows God. Whoever does not love does not know God, because God is love.'

The spirit mentioned in the very first chapter of the Bible is the spirit of the creator God, the spirit who breaths the life of

God into his Creation and into those humans who ask for it. This is the spirit which gives life to the people of God, the spirit which enables each part of God's Creation to be what it was created to be and enables each part of his Creation to integrate with the rest of the universe – the spirit of harmony, of shalom.

Why then is there so much emphasis on ecstatic experiences and strange language? This seems to me to derive from confusing the symptoms and the cause. Where people experience the presence of creative love they often respond in ecstasy – particularly in communities which have not developed a tradition of suppressing their feelings: 2,000 years later the more prosaic 20th century Anglo-Saxon culture looks back on the early Church and has difficulty in analyzing what they read. The mistake has been to confuse the symptom for the reality. Other cultures, other temperaments have their own ways of expressing delight and joy and there is a great need for mutual understanding.

But – as I said earlier – it seems to me that if we have a theology of guilt and redemption there is much less likely to be openness to God's Spirit of love, for love is generous and does not operate contractually. In this case we will be much more open to receive God's Spirit and realize that in so doing we are being breathed into by God and receiving his life and love. We are truly becoming made in his image again; sons and daughters of God.

Now humans have always been hooked on numbers and I suspect that the New Testament is no different from any other set of claims for the size of the crowd, the number of communicants, the numbers at the revival meeting, at the demonstration etc.. And of course we all round the numbers up or down, depending on our point of view. But here was a phenomenon which did not need numbers. Jesus cured individuals – he didn't have mass healings. Ten lepers who were cleansed is at the top end of the scale, and so many of those whom Jesus encountered and who were miraculously healed or changed were on their own. But when love is involved you only need one or two or three and they in their turn connect with their two or three and it takes off exponentially. That is why we hear of the 70s and the 5,000s and so on. And when it comes to those sorts of numbers there is always the danger that mass hysteria of some sort takes over and we have to go back to the beginning again with the ones and twos and threes.

Now all over the western world the Church has been fighting a losing battle for the hearts and minds of 20th century humans. The development of the sciences, the technological revolution, the liberation of women, the advent of weapons of mass destruction...these have all contributed to the abandonment of religious faith and observance. As a result the churches, many of which by now have built themselves into monolithic institutions, are suffering a marked decline in numbers and in influence. And, having generally lost their nerve, they are playing the numbers game for all they are worth.

The measure therefore of a successful church at the beginning of the 21st century is purely statistical. The aims of the Church in the 21st century are largely statistical, and didn't the Archbishop of Canterbury (no less) challenge all Anglican churches to increase their rolls by ten per cent?... A Biblical tithe, of course.

And of course we are all guilty of the numbers game. I have to confess that I presided over a falling roll in the Church where I was a vicar and I am quite sure that some of the blame for that lies at my door. The question is, however, what should be done about it?

One approach is to find out where the Church is succeeding, numerically, and adopt the same practices as they use.

Let us go along to St Andrews, in Home Counties commuter land. Built at the end of the 19th century, it holds just over 350 at a sitting. The vicar is in his late forties and has a teenage family. He is an articulate university graduate who worked as a marketing consultant until he was converted to Christ as the result of a series of lunchtime talks at the City church near his office. He has charm and is a persuasive speaker who is at ease with the modern world, yet he clearly has his sights on the Kingdom of God and its permanence in contrast with the transient nature of life on earth. He is good-looking, personable and has an easy manner in the pulpit. He has also spent a year with one of the well-known churches in the USA, learning the modern techniques of discipling. The leaders of St Andrews have a lot of experience in similar churches in the UK. They play on the fact that the perception of the Church by the non-churchgoer is that it is boring, too hidebound by tradition, that those who go are miserable people who wish they were still in the 19th century and that they hark back to the good old days of the Book of Common Prayer and the Authorized Version of the Bible. This not without some justification, for there are many country churches which – with the best will in the world – cannot drag themselves into the 21st century and who justify their torpor with the comment, 'It has stood the test of time,' notwithstanding the fact that there are few who go to Church.

But St Andrews has very definitely opted for the modern age. The vicar enters in smartish ordinary clothes: no robes, no dog collar. He puts people at ease with a warm welcome and a few humorous remarks. The service is very informal and takes the form of songs accompanied by a group consisting of keyboard, clarinet and guitars. There are three young women up front who lead the singing through a microphone. The singing is divided into well-known hymns which are played to a modern pop rhythm and what are termed worship songs – modern Christian music in the same idiom. The organ is not used. A male member of the congregation comes out in front to read part of one of St Paul's Letters, and there are many people in the congregation who follow in the numerous Bibles in the pews. After some more singing the vicar moves to the reading desk – the pulpit being too imposing to suit the relaxed and informal atmosphere. With his Bible in hand he introduces his theme: he runs through a number of illustrative anecdotes and highlights the difference between those who –though they would call themselves Christians – very seldom go to church and those who have had their lives changed by giving their lives to the living Jesus, and putting him at the very centre of all that they think and do.

The vicar is a very good preacher. He has a confident and easy manner, he is au fait with the modern teenager and the business executive as well as the harassed mother of three, and for him it seems that God is not a remote figure in the distance but a friend to whom he and even you can confide. He finishes his talk with a challenge to everyone to review and/or renew their commitment to Christ and to spread the Good News to those who have not heard it, and as you look at your watch you realize with surprise that he has been speaking for 40 minutes.

But he is just part of an atmosphere which is consistently warm, positive and unashamed about the importance of faith in Jesus, the Son of God. And it is no purely heavenly matter. It is very down to earth and particularly concerned with issues of personal morality and their relevance to the problems of the modern age. As you leave the packed church you are met with smiles from those around you, and at the door someone asks you if you are new and 'May we give you a leaflet about the Church for you to fill in at your leisure?'... And you are outside discovering that that there are people not only leaving the Church but walking towards it and you realize that there is another service soon after the one you have attended, such is the demand for this style of worship.

So you decide to go again – and feel just a tinge of guilt at not going more often to your local C of E church. But you have never liked the atmosphere there – it seems to be geared to people who have got stuck in the past, and the music is tired and the choir consists of four 50-plus ladies and two men of the same vintage. Besides…there is absolutely nothing specially geared to young people and now that your children have grown out of Sunday school this new church might be able to attract them, for there seems to be a thriving youth fellowship with a very lively young man working full time as a youth leader.

After three Sundays at St Andrews you are beginning to feel relaxed in the church. You have had a few chats with one of the mothers whom you knew by sight at the school car park and she has suggested that you might like to come along to one of the series of talks about parenting that the Church has arranged. Apparently the speaker is excellent and has spoken in churches all over the South east. You go along and enjoy the talks, though you feel that somehow the speaker is a little too confident that if you follow a particular line then your children will turn out as paragons of virtue and they will be converted to Christ in good time before leaving the nest and launching out into student life.

By this time you are well on the way to becoming a member of the Church. You have already been to one of the house groups which the school contact recommended; you have got to know her a lot better and are beginning to feel at home with the group you have joined.

At one of the meetings the subject of conversion has come

up and it transpires that most of those in the group can point to an occasion when they became Christian or – as some of them said – 'they gave their lives to Christ.' Now you know that you are a Christian – you have always felt deeply that there is a God and that Jesus somehow is the channel through which you find God, particularly when times are difficult – especially the time five years ago when your youngest had leukaemia. Your parents were Christians – they used to go regularly to church but things tailed off when Dad was posted abroad, and somehow they never got going again on returning to this country. But no parents could be more generous, both within the family and outside in the community.

Yet you begin to hear more and more this distinction between committed Christians and the sort that your parents seem to be. There is a most particular emphasis on committed Christians being prepared to talk about their faith and lead others to Christ. In fact you feel that once you sign up to being a committed Christian your job is to join the large number of people who are helping to tell the uncommitted all about your faith and what Jesus has done for you. That aside it really is refreshing to hear people talking quite openly about their faith – and clearly it means a lot to them and provides a focus for their lives, which you seem to lack. They make a lot of the difference that their new-found faith has made to their lives and they feel that they have an obligation to share their faith with others.

There is a very great emphasis on the Bible and it is plain that it is used as the basis for all questions on faith and right living. In fact the whole emphasis is on living a Christian life and witnessing to others through your actions. A great deal of the teaching of the Church is centred round the Christian life and the Bible underpins a clear-cut moral message with the neatly argued Biblical endorsement of a Christian's attitude to this issue or that. Invariably the ethical stances are clear-cut and they tend to concentrate on personal morals, family life and the individual conscience rather than community, national and global issues of poverty, justice, corruption and war.

To a large extent this is not too surprising since there is a great emphasis on beginning the faith and on the personal and therefore individual nature of its expression: for the same reason the exposition of the meaning of Biblical texts must not be too complex and there are many gifted speakers who make faith come alive – and whose persuasive exposition neatly clears up the issues for many people. For we live in an age where moral standards seem to change almost yearly, where each succeeding generation seems to have abandoned the values of its parents and there are no moral certainties any more. St Andrews and other churches like it are havens of well-established moral values and many people come to have these traditions upheld and encouraged, so they stand out as islands of morality in an increasingly anarchic and evil world. It is very easy (therefore) to see those who are outside your own particular church tradition as somewhat suspect and not wholly committed to the Gospel.

For you are now being taught to discern the hallmarks of the committed Christian: he or she has had a dramatic conversion experience, is very keen to share his or her faith with others and is very willing to witness to that conversion in public. He is submitting his name to candidature for ordination and is going to spend Christmas working in a soup kitchen in the inner city. He is getting to know the Bible very well and is able to quote from it, both during the prayer meeting and in general conversation. She is what is known as a super-Christian – a role model for those who are just setting out in their Christian life.

Now that is a bit unfair, for there are many people who will qualify for the above description who simply get on with their lives unselfconsciously – and their virtues are extolled by others and not by them. But where people are made self-conscious about their faith and an emphasis is put on witnessing to one's faith and moral issues are taken up over many different aspects of life – homosexuality, pre-marital sex, abortion, divorce, drug taking, the status of women – and the correct attitude to each marks you down as a committed Christian or not, then the faith ceases to be a Gospel and becomes much more a latter-day version of the law which enslaves.

So misleading is the word Christian these days that a very good discipline for Lent might be to ban its use and then we would have to think about what we really mean when we say things like: 'Britain is (or is not) a Christian country', 'she is not a very good Christian', 'that was not a very Christian action', for on almost every occasion we use the word as if it were a measure of how many percentage points we might earn in good deeds – and this seems to be one of the things which has turned the Christian religion from a religion of grace to a religion of effort.

But very seldom do we hear anyone saying that a Christian is someone who knows that they are a sinner, but that in Jesus God has fundamentally done something about it. It is precisely because we are a community of those who know their need of Christ – because of our sin – that we are able to accept each other as brothers and sisters.

Sadly, too, many Christians presume to judge other people's standing before God. Unless, they say, you express your belief as we do you can't call yourself a Christian. Unless you acknowledge the Bishop of Rome as head of the Church – unless you have had a conscious experience of conversion – unless you speak in tongues – unless you believe that homosexuality is a disease – unless you believe that the Bible is the sole authority of faith… But our commitment to Christ is partial – our understanding of Christ is incomplete – our capacity for receiving his spirit is limited. But still he persists in knocking on the door of our hearts and presenting himself as the one who includes rather than excludes.

Yet I and thousands of others owe a huge debt to an evangelical expression of faith, which challenged our complacency and confronted us with Jesus of Nazareth through the message of the Bible. And maybe we need a period when we see a contrast between the life of faith and the life without God to keep us on the rails until we are ready to trust to our own navigation. The temptation is to cling on to what we know and to put off or run away from the need to take our own route.

Years ago when I was little we used to play with friends across the road who had a pond in their garden. To me, at the age of seven or eight, the pond seemed large enough and we used to punt two rafts around and have imaginary battles against each other. There were no adults around but the pond was shallow and we came to no harm. Later on we progressed to a rowing skiff and a canoe on the river Avon. Like Ratty in Wind in the Willows I came to think that there was nothing quite so wonderful as simply messing about in boats. Unfortunately, soon after we moved to Yorkshire and then Hertfordshire – both of which precluded boating – except for three years in which I did some very amateur rowing for my Cambridge college.

Many years later (therefore) I was determined to acquire my own boat, which we used to tow around to various waters as far afield as the Solent, north Cornwall and the west of Scotland. But towing boats on motorways and launching them off exposed beaches tends to pall with increasing age (of the owner, not the boat) so on retirement we acquired a small cruiser which we keep on one of the east coast estuaries, with the intention of combining our interests in boating and bird watching.

Because it is substantially larger and heavier than the previous boats it displaces more water and needs a depth sounder. This has been quite restrictive, for we have failed as yet to find a chart of the estuary and so we have to grope our way along with one eye on the digital depth sounder. When we acquire the chart we shall proceed more confidently because we shall know where the deeper water is, but it will still restrict our ability to relax and look around us and find an appropriate anchorage from which to watch the ducks and waders.

Eventually, however, we shall become so familiar with the configuration of the estuary and the foibles of the boat that we shall be able to relax and be free to enjoy the beauty of the scenery and the peace of being out on the water.

The trouble is that in faith, as in sailing, there is always the temptation to play safe and deny ourselves the freedom that we could enjoy. On our journey of faith there are too many opportunities to be bogged down by charts and regulations and instrumental aids. There are too many people along the way who, from the best of intentions, nevertheless encourage us to stick to the rule book and the chart, at the expense of enjoying the freedom which our boat should give us. The essential thing is to know when is the right moment to take the plunge and to trust to your own judgement.

For some of the reasons that I have outlined above the evangelical expression of the Christian faith is fairly prescriptive. The faith is officially outlined in sets of theological propositions which become important on such occasions as choosing a candidate for a church post or a teaching position. But this produces a problem if we set it beside the personal nature of our relationship with God. And since the Reformed Church puts great store by justification by faith and not by works (Jesus's injunction to John's disciples to tell John what you see – that the lame walk, the blind see etc.) it does not seem to qualify as an authentication of faith. But being personal to me and God must mean that the relationship is unique and therefore will lead to a unique understanding and expression.

Sadly there is too much of a tendency to claim exclusive truth for evangelical theology and practice and to unchurch those who feel called to express their faith and worship God in different ways. The fact that the numerical growth of evangelical Christianity seems to be in the ascendance encourages its members to feel that they are right and that therefore those of a more individualistic, Catholic or liberal point of view are wrong.

Once again the problem arises because we talk in these absolute terms about an inexact science (theology). This is where Jesus's insistence that all have sinned could help different factions to share their common sinfulness and exchange their differing perspectives in a mutually constructive way.

But just as in the sailing analogy the key to all this is trust. We need to trust that our evangelical or liberal neighbour has a relationship with God just as we do. That in expressing our faith in the differing ways that we do actually enriches the Church rather than threatening it. And that by accepting that God's Holy Spirit will enter the lives of very different Christians from ourselves we can all be released from a spirit of rivalry, partisanship and judgement.

Now – if there is a lack of trust in the Church – how much more is that going to be apparent in society? This is why a feature of modern life is that we are being overrun with rules and regulations. When I first started out as a school teacher organizing and leading field study courses and expeditions the only rules were those of common sense. We took the number of supervising staff which seemed appropriate to the particular project concerned. Hygiene, medical precautions and safety precautions were not laid down in a book of rules but we always played safe, and I know that the young people from time to time thought that we were spoilsports.

Nowadays, partly because of various high profile accidents – but also substantially because of a breakdown of trust – supervising staff are confronted by reams of rules setting out numbers of staff, their qualifications to lead the group, children, medical and dietary details, forms of indemnity or permission signed by parents.

And – talking of schools – there is a complete lack of trust in teachers by parents and by government. As a result we have a situation in which the workload, already very heavy for the conscientious, has become intolerable. Society has decided that only the big sticks of inspection, the imposition of red tape and the fear of failure will turn the service round. As one who has spent a lifetime in schools (and two of my children are teachers) I am reaching the point where in conscience I would say, 'I wouldn't blame you for leaving the profession.'

I am sure that everyone has their own pet version of lack or betrayal of trust in life. Insurance of cars, houses, travel – and the crafty little disclaimers which, with the aid of a magnifying glass, you could just discern if you had the time to spend 20 to 30 minutes reading it. Employer rescinding promise of promotion made to worker. Politician reneging on manifesto. Householder insisting on estimates and penalty clauses. Ministry of Agriculture, Forestry and Fisheries insisting on minutely-detailed measurements of every field in a small highland farm, with draconian penalties for the smallest discrepancy. Gazumping. Husband walking out on wife after 32 years of marriage.

But trust, on the other hand, is part of what love is all about. It involves exposing one's inner self to another with no guarantee of response. It involves giving with no expectation of receiving back. It is a commitment far beyond the horizon of our experience. But it is the only thing that unlocks the love in others. For trust which, like love, is unconditional calls out the same from those who receive it.

Chapter 10

JUST GETTING FAT

When I met my wife it was not very long before I realised that we clicked. It wasn't that I was particularly attracted to her at that stage – it was just that she was fun, unpretentious and we found that we shared several of the same interests. As our relationship developed we began to talk more and more about things that mattered to us and as we did that we were drawn closer together – one of the results of which was my being challenged by the Gospel and the other that we got married.

This was one model of how the love of God can work. We talk a lot about our relationship with God, but when it comes to making connections – to spreading the Gospel – we downgrade that and almost equally talk in terms of campaigns and committees and courses and sermons.

If we accept that God is love – the love that in exchange enhances the value of each of the participating individuals – we will acknowledge that the Spirit of God is that catalyst, that ruach or breath which effects the exchange and the creation of new life – each for the other, and that in the same way that new life will be exchanged in turn with another and so the networks of relationship will build up until in any locality there is a small community of those whom God has transformed through the Holy Spirit of Jesus (whose Lordship is the focus for their lives and their ongoing relationships).

As they come together to break bread and receive his spirit anew they will also be challenged by the ministry of the Word and, as they meet Jesus again in the Gospel, so they will be acutely conscious of how little they love others in the light of his love and ministry to those whom he encountered. In their penitence they will recall their baptism and once again kneel in penitence to ask for and receive his absolution. But, transcending any sort of feelings of inadequacy or even guilt, they will also become aware of the generosity of God and the promises he holds out 'to make all things new'.

As they then continue along their daily lives they will in their turn seek to love their fellow humans (whom they will see as fellow pilgrims) who have needs that they can meet. Because of the bond of their common humanity there will be no sense of otherness because of their Christian faith, for they remember the words of Jesus when he said, 'Inasmuch as you did it to one of these, the least of my brethren, you did it to me.' Yet relationships will develop in the fertile soil of love and, where there is a spirit of enquiry and of seeking, so will faith develop and grow. As individuals are drawn into the Church, so they will experience – maybe just once, maybe more drawn out – the same sort of elation which overcame the disciples at Pentecost, but probably in a very much more restrained manner (though much later they may look back on it with a much greater feeling of elation).

So they will continue this cycle of love and relationship and seeking and experiencing the joy of faith in Jesus Christ.

Now, of course, all of this needs fleshing out to give it even a semblance of reality, and the Church which applies this sort of model to itself will most probably already have a history and a body of tradition which means that there is a lot of baggage which will compromise the situation. But then we are of course concerned with the real world and as I have said before, the great thing about heaven is that there will be no need for religion there.

So to bring us down to earth we will go to St Cuthberts. It was built in 1887 in a Midlands industrial town which had seen phenomenal growth throughout the Industrial Revolution but, being Church of England, we had to wait for a decent space of time before the realization that half the English population had moved to the towns. By this time the Oxford Movement had stimulated a revival of Catholic theology and liturgy and the worship of the Church was given its pattern by the liturgical year and a focus on the sacraments. Fortunately it has discarded the worst features of the old-fashioned High Church, and the Second Vatican Council and Common Worship have combined to fashion a more humane religion. The congregation is very mixed, for while there is a substantial element of old inhabitants who live in the turn of the century villas a lot of these villas are being bought up now by young professional/technocrat families who are also moving into the upmarket housing estates springing up on the nearby abandoned sites of the Victorian factories.

The main service of the week is the Sunday Eucharist – which is beginning to come to grips with Common Worship now that the congregation has realised that it is almost indistinguishable from ASB Rite A. And the settings and hymns are a judicious mixture of old and new, since while there are not very many young families as yet there are several who are very serious about their faith and the vicar doesn't want the traditionalists to discourage them.

What might be called the outreach of the Church is centred on the occasional Offices – in other words baptisms, weddings and funerals – but it is rather more all-embracing, effectively, since it includes anyone in need. However, the recognition that people often start to ask serious questions at these rites of passage gives the Church opportunities to make the connections between people's deepest feelings and the love of God.

St Cuthberts runs a mums and babies group which is open to all members of the community, and there is no requirement or expectation that families should come to church or even be interested in the faith. In practice, however, the Church makes sure that church members are involved in the organization and the vicar regularly spends time talking to mothers, grannies and childminders. By this route a significant number of families are drawn into the Church with what is probably a fairly average proportion of eventual regular, sporadic and rare attenders. Preparation for baptism is taken very seriously and the vicar or some qualified lay person visits families in their homes. The baptism takes place during one of the main Sunday Eucharists with the congregation swollen by visiting godparents, relations and friends. The church takes the line that the sacrament expresses the faith and duties of the Church, and assumes that the parents' willingness to publicly express their faith is a token of their commitment.

From the above description it can be seen that St Cuthberts has a significant if unimpressive number of regular worshippers. Anything over 60 communicants is a good number – not counting the addition of baptism parties – most of whom find it difficult to accept the invitation to the altar for the sacrament or a blessing. Of these the most regular are in their 50s and 60s and provide the core of the membership and a majority of the executive. This is the section of the Church which knows each other most intimately so that there is a danger in that their very intimacy creates a barrier for those who might be tempted to dip their toe into church life.

St Cuthberts' policy is that in welcoming newcomers they assume that everyone is in until they declare themselves out. Applied to the life of the previously-mentioned St Andrews it could be said that they assumed people were out unless and until they declare themselves in.

There is a further comparison that characterizes churches such as those we have been examining. The St Andrews model would see themselves as a community called out of the world to witness to the truth of the Gospel of Christ who saves us from our sins and makes us righteous before God. The Cuthbertians would perhaps perceive their role as being essentially part of the community of human sinners in their particular locality but also bearers of love within that community and making the connection for those whom they serve and the God whom they know in Jesus.

Because their tradition has been a sacramental one there is less emphasis on the Bible and members are very much less confident about expressing their beliefs and encouraging others in the religious expression of their faith. There is very much less study and prayer activity and many more purely social gatherings such as quizzes, bazaars, barbecues and hikes. It is probably this that has given St Cuthberts something of a reputation as a clique.

But due to its size, the church cannot provide what might be seen as a comprehensive ministry to the community. There is a Sunday school which takes place during the ministry of the Word in church but its numbers and facilities mean that it is difficult to set up an appropriate course, and the dearth of teachers means there is too little continuity to build relationships between church members and their young people.

However, opportunities to serve in the sanctuary and assist in other ways mean that there are opportunities for relationships across and between all the generations before the Devil – in the guise of mini rugby and horse riding and GCSE coursework – enters the fray.

Just a few yards away from the church is the C of E primary

school, of which the vicar is chairman of governors. It is a popular school in the neighbourhood and there is a danger of it becoming too selective because of the lengths to which prospective parents will go to gain entry for their offspring, with the usual flurry of churchgoing as school age approaches. The vicar is acutely aware that most of the avowed Anglicans who are desperate for their offspring to gain entry will fall away in their churchgoing after successfully negotiating the entry obstacles, but the last thing he wants to do is to put any kind of test of faith on anyone. However, he also sees how difficult the conflict is between his duty to his own parishioners – who may not necessarily be Christian – and those whose convictions bring them to a school which is avowedly church-based in teaching and ethos, whatever the latter means.

But, like so many churches, St Cuthberts is continually concerned about money. The town is not a particularly wealthy one and such endowments which derive from the medieval history of the area go to the old parish church in the centre of town. There have been a few bequests but they come nowhere near being a substantial help. So there is always pressure to build up numbers – to put bums on seats. Traditionally, the church has used conventional means of fund-raising, such as bazaars and raffles; sponsored everything from Bible reading through anthem singing to lengths of the primary school's 15-metre pool – 107 lengths to the mile.

And to set each of these up there has to be a committee, with its chair reporting back to the PCC with recommendations for them to endorse. However, this does not save time (as one might thin) because the whole issue is dissected in committee and the meeting typically ends up finishing at 11.10pm. Of course, we are told that all these activities generate fellowship. Whether they always generate loving relationships is another matter.

Years ago, at an early stage of my journey, I read a couple of books by a South American pastor called Juan Carlos Ortiz. In his book *Disciple* he describes how when he went to work in Buenos Aires it was not long before his congregation had grown from 1884 members to over 600. He describes some of the things which this involved and then writes as follows...

'Yet underneath it all I sensed that something wasn't right. Things seemed to stay high so long as I worked 16 hours a day. But when I relaxed everything came down. That disturbed me. Finally, I decided to stop. I told my board, '...I must go away for two weeks to pray.' I headed for the countryside and gave myself to meditation and prayer.

The Holy Spirit began to break me down. The first thing he said was, 'Juan, that thing you have is not a church. It's a business.'

I didn't understand what he meant.

'...You are promoting the Gospel the same way Coca-Cola sells Coke,' he said, 'the same way Reader's Digest sells books and magazines. You are using all the human tricks you learned in school. But where is my hand in all of this?'

I didn't know what to say. I had to admit that my congregation was more of a business enterprise than a spiritual body.

Then the Lord told me a second thing. 'You are not growing,' he said. 'You think you are, because you've gone from 200 to 600. But you're not growing – you're just getting fat.'

Now there was never any danger of St Cuthberts trebling its numbers, but there are parallels perhaps with the picture that I have painted of St Andrews in the previous chapter.

The feature which is common to all three is that it is just

too easy to get into the trap of making numerical growth the touchstone of spiritual progress. There is no evidence that Jesus was concerned about numbers. If he had been I think his ministry would have been radically different. He knew that by spending time with people such as Zacchaeus, Mary Magdalene, the centurion, his disciples, he was enabling the Spirit of God to work its miracles of translating from person to person. When large numbers were involved it was not of Christ's doing, but finding himself so surrounded he responded to their need and fed them.

And here is the dilemma faced by so many church leaders. We want to be unworldly; we want to spend our time with the frailest and most inconsequential members of the community; yet we also find ourselves adjusting to the modern order and going along with its priorities so too much of our time is spent with the great and the good, the wealthy and the influential.

Here in rural Suffolk our village is large enough to have a fair range of services but the village shop has only recently been revitalized by the arrival of a new owner from Harrow who originates from India and who is literally open all hours, with a significantly wider range of goods than before. Along with the two pubs, the post office and the infant school the village is well provided for, with a real focus for the community. The two villages immediately adjacent to ours, however, have lost all their services. There is no longer a shop in Shop Close, and not even a vestige of a pub in one village. In the other the village school has become a rather grand private home: there is no pub and the part-time post office is now closed for good.

It should not be too surprising that the Church is tempted to follow a very similar pattern of development. It is all too easy to use the same techniques for marketing the Christian faith as retailers use. Economies of scale mean that in a central location different tastes can be satisfied over a wide catchment area. The commodities can be standardized and attractively packaged. This is accomplished by ignoring the existent traditional market and going for the modern attractive eye- and ear-catching style of church. Traditional hymns and songs are either abandoned or packaged with pop rhythms. The clergy discard traditional liturgical robes and dress casually in slacks and jacket.

Theology is downgraded and simple propositions and a particular tradition of scriptural interpretation are the vehicles for inculcating faith, and these are fiercely guarded and upheld by the leadership. The greatest emphasis is on a defence of certain traditional moral stances, particularly in the area of personal and sexual morality. So as with St Andrews there is a dangerous tie-up between this style of Christianity and western right-wing laissez-faire politics.

And lest I be accused of any sort of bigotry I quote a respected evangelical theologian and teacher who is reported as saying that there would be a handful of mega-churches. These would be entrepreneurial and take up advertising and marketing, but also make use of management consultants. He said that smaller churches might be nervous of this but the Church had to listen to people outside, however difficult and painful that might be.

But so what? On the other side we have the loony left. They are typified by liberal theologians who all but abandon any sort of faith which calls for trust rather than intellectual assent. They are led by people who seem to believe in figments of their own imagination and projections of debatable psychological theories. Their congregations are little more than inward-looking religious clubs which are concerned only for their own members, and their liturgies and music are still stuck in the past.

So: the Evangelicals look down on the liberals and the liberals are frightened of the Evangelicals and everyone has forgotten St Paul's letter to the Corinthians:

> *'Brothers, I could not address you as spiritual but as worldly – mere infants in Christ. I gave you milk, not solid food, for you were not yet ready for it. Indeed, you are still not ready. You are still worldly. For since there is jealousy and quarrelling among you, are you not worldly? Are you not acting like mere men? For when one says, "I follow Paul", and another, "I follow Apollos", are you not mere men? What, after all, is Apollos? And what is Paul? Only servants, through whom you came to believe – as the Lord has assigned to each his task. I planted the seed, Apollos watered it, but God made it grow. So neither he who plants nor he who waters is anything, but only God, who makes things grow.'*

I have commented earlier on the tendency of parts of the Church to draw lines between believers and unbelievers, pseudo-believers and semi-believers and many of us have been confused at some time or another as to where the truth could be found on this. One wise priest giving a lunchtime Lent talk shed a lot of light on the issue. He said that people tend to think of Christian or religious differences as between conservatives and liberals, Catholics and Protestants, west and east, Anglican and Nonconformist. The significant dividing line, he said, is between those who are open Christians and those who are closed. The closed Christians have worked out their theology to their satisfaction and defend it for all that they are worth. Their beliefs are set in stone and encapsulate the complete truth of God in Christ: they are the last word in theological exposition. The open Christians (with St Paul) believe that, *'Now we see but a poor reflection as in a mirror; then we shall see face to face. Now I know in part; then I shall know fully, even as I am fully known.'*

And yet there are still some theological colleges which are still organized and taught from one particular tradition, with little attempt at objective assessment of those who differ in their views. I remember a young man accepted for ordination training waiting to hear whether the vacant principal's appointment in a particular college would go to someone whose theology he endorsed. But the cost of full-time college training is becoming more and more of a stumbling block and, increasingly, courses are based on diocesan needs and attended by ordinands from every tradition. I well remember at one of our long residential courses a contentious issue being over a planned service of benediction, which Protestants have traditionally rejected as idolatry. It provoked a huge amount of heat and not a little anger, but nevertheless it produced a great widening of most people's perception as well as the warmth of the ensuing reconciliation. It made us all think and drew us all a bit closer.

The trouble so often is that those who believe in everything, so to speak, tend to think that most others believe in nothing. Yet Jesus said, *'I tell you the truth. If you have faith as small as a mustard seed you can say to this mountain, "Move from here to there" and it will move. Nothing will be impossible for you.'*

In fact it seems quite likely that Jesus's mission was simply to open up the Jewish understanding of their faith. It is so often the case that when people are on the defensive they become too aware of the differences between themselves and others, rather than their common heritage. And Jesus lived at such a time, shortly after the persecutions of Antiochus and the subsequent Roman conquest.

In any case, the evidence suggests that most of what we quarrel about is so much hot air. This was brought home to me when I was happy to assume that anyone who was not evangelical was suspect, if not a non-believer. I had read quite a few biographies of outstanding Christian witnesses from people such as Luther to John Wesley and the founder of the China Inland Mission, Hudson Taylor. I had been particularly captivated by the story of Gladys Aylward (a most unlikely candidate for the mission field) who failed in her application but was so determined to get to China from where she believed God was calling her that she saved up her pay as a ladies' maid and went the cheapest way – overland – via Russia and Japan (who were at war with each other. She actually crossed the no-man's-land between the two sides on foot. Eventually reaching China, she soon found herself involved in the results of the Sino-Japanese war of 1937 – 1945, collecting sensitive information for China and eventually leading 100 children to safety across an exposed mountain range. While her avowed mission was to bring salvation to the Chinese people her approach to this was essentially practical and her evangelism was rooted in a transparent love for the people among whom she lived and worked.

Years later she was in England recounting her exploits and experiences to churches and other Christian groups, and her autograph consisted of the words *Jesus is love* written in English and in Chinese characters.

Yet another person whose life I admired was Mother Teresa of Calcutta who though she had gone out to India from Bulgaria with a community of nuns to educate the daughters of wealthy Indians she discovered her true mission in those she found abandoned and dying on the streets of Calcutta. Her avowed aim to enable people to die with dignity and care and the growth and development of this mission is one of the most heart-warming stories of the 20th century.

But it was her story in particular which persuaded me that our divisions are not God's will. For if a Roman Catholic could demonstrate the character of Jesus in her life, then the Protestant strictures over Catholic theology and Church law were revealed for what they are – party stipulations and almost nothing to do with the Gospel. In the eternal scheme of things they are inconsequential, and yet they cause untold misery quite unnecessarily because of the insecurity of the Catholic Church and of the Protestant groups who oppose them.

Finally I was greatly moved by the story of Ernest Gordon, the Scottish soldier who was captured by the Japanese during the Second World War. He describes the appalling conditions and the destruction of the prisoners' morale under the privations to which they were subjected. But here and there he encounters beacons of hope, and they turned out to be the product of the deep Christian hope of one or two individuals who made it their business to bring the love of God to those who were sick or dying or sunk in the depths of despair. Here there was no possibility of faith being other than real, or it was nothing. Here it showed itself in the simple down to earth self-sacrificial service of one man to another in need, and people made up their own minds as they saw the real connection between these men's deeds and their faith – they were all of a piece and therefore utterly convincing.

But mostly our witness and our service are deeply compromised and we catch ourselves being self-righteous, self-centred or downright unkind. How can God break through with these destructive influences at work? The good news is that somehow Jesus is able to cauterise the more pernicious teachings of the different churches and to enable their members to rise above their squabbles and their own self-centredness to receive the spirit of Jesus himself, through which they serve the needy.

Frankly I don't want to see churches full to overflowing, because it would mean that there was a superficial attraction – an easy message – through which those who want a quick fix can find it (for a little while). Neither do I want to see church communities spending the whole of their lives in church activities and enticing others to come and join them.

What I really want is an invisible church: a church that you don't see in action because its ministry is substantially one-to-one – doing very mundane things to help, support and encourage their neighbours to see how good God is and what a wonderful world we live in.

Occasionally there will be visiting speakers and there will be issues which need to be addressed by the Church coming together to share concerns and ideas but by and large we should want to cut out a lot of the religious activity, which can so easily cease to be a faith and become a hobby.

Most people will come just once a week to the main Eucharist. The call to repentance and the confession will remind everyone of their common human condition of selfishness and sin; then they will have their eyes opened a bit more through the encouraging exposition of the Bible and another window on to the man Jesus. Then comes the timeless drama of the Eucharist, which is re-enacted with great simplicity but with real devotion by all those involved. And because of the power of symbols to communicate the most profound truths so will the very varied characters – who make up the congregation – receive the truth of God incarnate in their fashion and degree of understanding. As they stand round the altar to receive the sacrament so Jesus will be made present for them, for the worshipping community, and then he will go out in the love of his servants to heal the wounds of the world.

Finally, they will pray for God's blessing and then, some quickly and some very slowly, they will leave the church and make their way to their own patch – and they will be such a mixed bunch of people. Responsible and wealthy businessmen and women; single mothers with their obstreperous toddlers; the widows of factory workers struck down by occupational diseases; hopeful Oxbridge candidates and season ticket holders at the jobcentre. And the mix takes account of their faith journeys, which range from those who find it difficult to do anything more than focus on a very vague image of Jesus to those who are tussling with very complicated theology; from those whose prayer life is regular and nourishing to those who go for weeks without a single thought of God.

But the one thing they have in common is that they are drawn to this church because they feel included, even if they hardly ever make it through the door; because the person of Jesus is made to come alive; because there is a spirit of hope and trust in the goodness of God; and perhaps more than anything else they feel free to be themselves with all their doubts, their fears and their inadequacies.

Leaving aside the unlikelihood of such a church existing in even a near-perfect world, I very much doubt whether anyone would have the required courage and persistence to go against the flow. For a start the vicar would become a pretty unpopular figure among fellow ministers for being so isolationist. St Blanks would send so few people to deanery and diocesan committees that the Church's views would not feature beyond its own committees and fund-raising would present a real problem, with the committee being so uninterested in an outreach campaign.

But of one thing I am quite sure and that is that if we are concerned to make Jesus come alive to other people, first and foremost by loving them and also by putting them in the way of receiving him, then we need have no worries at all for the future. More than that – we can have a glorious hope.

Chapter 11

RELIGION OR FAITH?

It seems to have been a commonly accepted view that when you went into the army – or, for that matter, the navy or air force – you would be asked what religion you were. If you didn't know the answer, or didn't even understand the question, the sergeant would write down C of E against your name and you therefore could not escape church parades until you returned to civvy street.

I knew that we were strange, for we were Unitarians and the only thing I knew about that was concerned with the beliefs which they rejected. So, they didn't believe that Jesus was more than a very good human being and teacher, and that he was not the Son of God, and we did not say any sort of creed. My mother explained it succinctly when, quoting her grandfather, she described Unitarianism as a sort of "reverend agnosticism". It also became apparent that we didn't believe much in going to church either, until my brother and I started singing in the Church of England school chapel choir when we were well into our teens.

We had also come across those who were even further divorced from English religion, and these were school fellows from Jewish families at our Yorkshire grammar school. Quite understandably, they had a tendency to stick together, which was really no more significant than any other interest group, though perhaps their concession for being allowed off school on Saturdays might have been contentious if we had thought about it.

But I was really challenged later on when I arrived in Cambridge. During my first interview with the college Dean, the late Bishop Hugh Montefiore, his comment on hearing me describe myself as Unitarian produced the rejoinder, "Well they aren't Christians." My "indeed they are!" owed more to family loyalty than any clear understanding of the issues, and since then I have oscillated in my opinion depending to some extent on whether I was taking a theological or pastoral point of view.

In my twenties, with my new-found Christian faith, I was quite ready to throw over my family allegiance and make it clear that I had moved from no faith to total faith. With the emphasis on witnessing to ones faith constantly held up to me, I am quite sure that I was something of a religious prig to my family. It wasn't until I found myself on the receiving end of other Christians' similarly discriminating judgement that I began to be a little less critical myself.

One of the things that happened as a result was to look back at my own progression to faith and realise that I was much more indebted to my family than I had previously thought. One of the hallmarks of both sides of my family was their very independent, and mainly liberal, approach to intellectual and political matters, which led me always to question established and accepted opinions and beliefs. Looking back, my encounter with the Gospels owed a great deal to this, and it would be fair to say that I was already being converted well before my conscious and public avowal of the Trinitarian faith.

So it was against this background that I had to make up my mind about the very high profile stance which foreign missions took in our church. Supporting foreign missions and sending out missionaries seemed to be the ultimate in Christian service, and anyone who was so involved was put on something of a pedestal. A very substantial proportion of the Church's income was devoted to this cause and we supported individuals in a variety of foreign locations. There was some tension at that time between the traditional support which we gave to societies, such as the Church Missionary Society, and more recent non-denominational ones, such as Wycliffe Bible Translators. Worthy as this work was, there were some situations which suggested that the kudos of being a missionary attracted some people for the wrong reasons and one family, which found themselves on hard times in this country, realised too late that their escape from financial difficulties was only achieved at considerable cost to their children's security and future prospects.

But against this, we also got to know some marvellous people, and generally our experience that those who were involved first hand in foreign missions were among the most tolerant and non-judgemental people you could find. Tony, who had spent years training teachers under the auspices of CMS in Nigeria, explained his approach to the many Muslims and adherents of other faiths in terms the landscape around him. His Christian faith was analogous to climbing a hill which enabled him to see the beauty of the scenery and the way before him which would take him to his destination. There would be others on other hills with their special views, all he felt prepared to say was, 'if you are lost and want to know the way come up this hill, I will show you my view and my route'. Since he had not been up any of the other hills, he could not comment on them: he could only speak from his own experience.

Another from the same society was Oliver Allison, Bishop of the Sudan. He had been there since the 1930s and left in the 1970s when he was succeeded by an African Bishop. The conduct of his ministry had been such that he was accepted by the Muslim government in the north as well as by the Christian rebels in the south, and he helped to achieve, what sadly turned out to be, a temporary cessation of hostilities. He was one of the friendliest, but most outspoken, people I have come across and he went down very well with the cynical secondary school boys to whom he spoke. He didn't go down quite so well when he was ticketed by an overzealous police-man for parking in a private cul-de-sac facing the wrong way with no lights. He stormed down to the police station and interviewed a somewhat nervous sergeant. "Sorry, sir. We were only doing our duty." Back came the retort, "That's what the Roman soldiers said when they crucified Jesus!"

The people I have mentioned have very clearly been those who worked in the mission field because they truly wanted to save those who, for lack of knowing Jesus, would be consigned to everlasting damnation. For years and years this had been the stimulus for evangelisation and its militant wing, the mediaeval Crusades. But within this generality, one can distinguish between those who wanted their personal and national religion and way of life to prevail, and those who had a genuine concern for the situation of those in other lands whose lack of faith put them in a precarious situation. As we look right back at the history of the Christian attitude to other faiths, we come across some terrible stories.

Perhaps one of the worst from the English point of view is the treatment of the Jews in the Middle Ages. They arrived in this country with the Norman invaders, who, being Christian, were not allowed to lend money on interest. The Jews, who had no such scruples, had become the money lenders of Europe and not surprisingly attained a position of wealth and influence. It was said that Aaron of Lincoln was so rich that he was even richer than the King. The Jews position was obviously safe until they started to call in their loans and as that happened, so animosity developed and their debtors began to look for ways of demonising them. This was not at all difficult, because of the unfortunate way in which the evils of a section of the Jewish establishment in Christ's time were attributed to 'the Jews' who, as a result, became collectively branded as Christ killers. As the debts owed to them became bigger, so stories of their alleged wickedness became more numerous and horrific and unscrupulous people took advantage of popular resentment to renege on their debts, to encourage persecution and even inflict physical harm. Perhaps the worst incidents occurred in York when harassed Jews took refuge in a tower, and rather than be killed by the mob for refusing to be baptised suffered excruciating death when the tower was set on fire. Such survivors, as there were, who had agreed to become Christians were butchered when they emerged from the tower. In London, there was a similar slaughter of Jews provoked by the appearance of some Jews supposedly illegally at King Richards celebrations.

It is very difficult for us to even contemplate the mindset of someone who knows that they are 'Christian' yet who can believe that it was right to threaten death to people who would not convert to the Christian faith. Equally terrible stories are known about the catholic conquistadores of the New World and the horrors inflicted on the 'infidels' of the Holy Land.

The position of the Jews became so bad that eventually they were expelled from England in 1290, not to return for another four hundred years.

The 19th century missionary bonanza was much more benign but, not surprisingly, very imperialist in its attitude to the converts. There was very little appreciation of the cultural differences of the peoples whom they were evangelising and far too much assumption that 19th century English values were synonymous with Christian living wherever they might be. However, the British administrations in places like India and Africa were far more enlightened than many other countries involved in the European colonial free-for-all. There were many great educational and medical institutions set up as part of the Christian mission to these areas, and however wrong their policies might have seemed with hindsight, for their time, they were as enlightened as one could expect.

But after the Second World War, the influx of a large number of immigrants and their respective faiths, religious education could no longer narrowly teach the literature and the theologies of Christianity and a much broader comparative religion of the main faiths and moral teachings developed. So now in teaching religious studies one is supposed to be objective, and it is especially serious to try to proselytise one's own religion. But if religion is anything, it is biased and subjective. One only has to attempt to imagine a teacher of some other subject saying, for instance, 'We shall study the following authors: Shakespeare, Milton, Dryden and Matthew Arnold. Here are the facts about them. I am not allowed to express an opinion; you must make up your own mind.'

However, as Chaplain I had an advantage for I could declare my bias by wearing my clerical collar – I was allowed to be subjective. But looking through my teaching outlines of ten years ago, I am reminded of how superficial our coverage of the world religions was and how very little, I suspect, of the content would be remembered now by those young people, now in their early thirties. But what did have an impact was that there was a small but significant representation of the main world religions in just about each class. So the pattern for each class of twenty-five was something like: seventeen British agnostics, two church-going Christians, three Muslims, two Hindus and one Jew. Inevitably, we used to invite representatives of each faith to describe religious activities and express their opinions. So we had graphic descriptions of these young people's experiences of attempting to keep the month of Ramadan, with the difficulties of observing the Fast, and their inevitable compromises; of one young lady's adventure on the Hajj; of the Jewish determination to get to Schule on Saturday afternoons, and the very much more inclusive religious outlook of the Hindus, despite their exotic celebrations and varied expressions of deity.

From time to time, these different faiths would be further revealed by encounters with parents which provided some of the context for the children's outlook.

What emerged from all this was not so much the differences of culture and country, but the universal nature of the different approaches to faith. To put it simply, in each faith there seemed to be those who used religion to exclude others and to command unquestioning acquiescence from their adherents, and others whose outlook was accepting and open in their relationships with others.

Perhaps the most high profile and recent example of this has been the tremendous spotlight that has been trained on the religion of Islam, particularly involving the Arab nations. Here, different interpretations of the faith have sought to justify the appalling events of September 11th 2001, and the style of religious observance and expression which has characterised those who are conducting a Jihad, a holy war, against the United States, and those who have accommodated their policies to those of the western world, or have nothing to gain and everything to lose by opposing that country.

There is nothing new in this and past centuries have witnessed the way in which the claims of one religion have been endorsed by the military actions of its adherents. In

recent years, however, with the growth of pluralist popula-
tions in many countries of the world, such conflicts would be
as likely to destroy a country from within rather than establish its superiority over any other.

And yet we are told in the Gospels, in the words of Jesus,
"Go into all the world and preach the good news to all creation. Whoever believes and is baptized will be saved, but
whoever does not believe will be condemned."

Here is an unequivocal command: it would seem to try to
get people of the Jewish, Muslim, Hindu, Sikh or Buddhist
faith to give up their religion and convert to the religion of
Jesus. Yet because of the coercion of states; of individuals;
of any with superior power or position to convert to the
Christian faith, from the middle ages to the twentieth century,
so I believe we have forfeited any right to claim superiority
for our religion in the popular sense of the word.

What I believe is required of us, is that we are called to
love all people on their terms and not on ours. The good news,
after all, is that God is a God who so values his creation that
he waits with open arms to receive those who turn back to
their Creator and seek to do his will. He is a God who seeks to
reconnect those who have broken their relationship with their
fellow humans, and with their creator and all of his creation.
But unless the Good News is lived first without any ulterior
motive, there really is no point at all in the religious posturing
that comes so easily to us.

And because we have made such a mess of the Good
News, because in so many ways we have contradicted what
Jesus is all about, we have to make sure that our currency
is not in words and philosophies, in rank and in power, but
in living out the command to love our neighbour as ourself.
And we shall do so, not with any sense of superiority of our
faith, but with a great sense of penitence for our blindness

and unkindness in the past and the present, and a hope for the future which acknowledges our dependence on God. We shall come together with our Muslim or Sikh friend whose problems, or loneliness, or fear we have shared, to learn more about God as we receive from those to whom we thought we could only give.

Grace is in her seventies now. When she was three she, along with her twin sister Eunice, were brought over to England as part of the Kindertransport whereby hundreds of Jewish children were rescued before they could be sent to the gas ovens of Auschwitz and other centres of the Holocaust. They were adopted by a Welsh Baptist minister and his wife who were childless, and brought up as if they were their natural children. Their original names and their parents' identity and location were concealed. At an early age, Eunice contracted a crippling condition which meant her being kept at home to be nursed. Grace was sent to boarding school and then trained as a nurse. Her adoptive father was very possessive of her and saw to it that any potential suitors were discouraged. It later came to light that he had been abusing her sexually for years, until she finally extracted herself from his dominance and got married.

When she was in her early fifties, she heard on the radio a report of a reunion for those who had been Kindertransport refugees at the beginning of the war. By that time she knew that her earliest years had been in a different identity and that she and her sister had been adopted by her 'parents'. She got in touch with the lady who made the broadcast and gradually, through persistent enquiries, established that her mother was Jewish, unmarried, and had been working as a domestic servant for wealthy families in Munich. As she unearthed more and more, she discovered that her father was a German soldier and that she and her sister were the product of a casual relationship between them. When she became pregnant he abandoned her and she became doubly vulnerable as an unmarried Jewish mother while he, the father, was not only a gentile, but a soldier of the Reich which later sent her mother to the gas chamber. Her origins were a mixture of tragedy and shame. Her name was really Susi Bechhofer. She discovered not only that she had a complete family of Orthodox Jews in New York, but that she also had a half-sister in East Germany, and that her father had died not long before.

Yet in spite of her abuse from her minister father, she was a Christian, almost certainly because of her experience of the care from certain members of staff of her boarding school: especially those who knew a little of her background. But she also felt very strongly that she had to honour her mothers' memory and to make up for the lack of support in those years of Nazi Germany. So she sought out her family in New York and embarked on a series of visits which re-established her relationship in spite of the shame that the family had suffered. She is Jewish and she is Christian, and although in one sense this is a contradiction, one cannot help feeling that she is nearer to what Jesus might have envisaged than the mutually exclusive traditions of the last two thousand years.

When Susi's story was broadcast by two national TV programmes, she experienced both sympathy and interest from some quarters, but also criticism from others. But due to the increased interest by the Church in the Jewish foundations of the Christian faith, she was invited to speak at a re-enactment of a Passover meal arranged by a Church as an alternative to what had become a rather tired repeat of the Maundy Thursday celebration of the Last Supper with Foot

Washing. The preparation for this event involved going to one of the nearby Synagogues (Liberal or Reformed) to receive theological and practical guidance from the Rabbi there.

In this experience, we had a real sense of what the Letter to the Hebrews expresses when we read – "For here we do not have an enduring city, but we are looking for the city that is to come." When we exchange thoughts and feelings with those from other faiths we cannot avoid being aware of two things above all others. The first is that it is quite impossible to really understand the point of view, but also the feelings of those whose journey has been fundamentally different from our own. The second is that if we only scratch the surface of the history of our respective faiths; we cannot fail to become aware of the way in which our own faith has been distorted and compromised in the eyes of others. How very much more apt to these present religious circumstances is Christ's (yes and Leviticus') injunction – "you must love your neighbour as yourself." And, of course, your neighbour turns out not to be a drug addict, or a mugger, or a teddy boy, or any other contemporary version of the rejects of society, but someone from a different faith, someone who has compromised the traditional more rigid faith of the community.

There is especial danger where there is an organic connection between the Church and the State as there is in the British Isles. Where the State, in the form of the Monarch and the Parliament, have the last word in the government of the Church, there is bound to be a tendency for the Gospel to be compromised. Where this is reflected in the still potent system of patronage, or in the suffocated ministry of many independent school chaplaincies there is a clear need for reform. The argument that establishment prevents the Church of England from being a sect as opposed to a national church is too often contradicted by the increasing exclusivism that is apparent, as faith becomes more and more an individual rather than a community affair.

It would seem, perhaps, that I am advocating a faith which has no confidence in itself, and which understands itself as purely relative to its environment, rather than as a belief system which claims to be the only revelation of the truth about God. Though I would express myself differently nothing could be further from the truth. I repeat my own testimony by saying that Jesus of Nazareth, the Son of God, changed my life completely and still is, and still can, be truly the Saviour of the world. But while, for me, he is the Sign and the focus of what the Creator God and his creation is all about, I cannot see any boundaries which can be drawn by humans without restricting the love of which Jesus is the ultimate expression. He is the light of the world – to understand the world and to see our way around it, we need to approach the light and hold our lives up to its radiance, but while it is easy to allow a shadow to fall upon us, because we are out of the direct line of his light, there is still light available from the reflection of other objects.

Twenty miles away to my right I can see the outline of Ely Cathedral silhouetted against the sky. It is one sign, though a very powerful one, of the Jesus whom I worship. Nearer home I like to take the opportunity of going into the Cathedral in Bury St Edmunds. Its Millennium project has been the building of a central tower, which, for historical reasons, was never completed before. And then still nearer there are the five churches of our benefice. By turns they, and the activities and people involved, all uplift me and infuriate me – just as I am quite sure that I do them. Yet they, and we, all represent the Body of Christ, the living presence of the Spirit of Jesus on this planet, and the promise of God to bring new life to his people and his creation. From time to time I wobble, but looking back it has been the abiding constant in my adult life, and one that I want to share more than anything else.

Once again, I find myself referring to the Samaritan woman at the well. After she and Jesus have had their exchange about the literal and symbolic references to water, she changes tack to contrast the different focuses of their respective religions. Jesus replies – "Believe me, woman, a time is coming when you will worship the Father neither on this mountain nor in Jerusalem. You Samaritans worship what you do not know; we worship what we do know, for salvation is from the Jews. Yet a time is coming and has now come when the true worshipers will worship the Father in spirit and truth, for they are the kind of worshipers the Father seeks."

It seems to me that many different religions have insights into the truth, but also feel the need to prescribe its limits and boundaries; to draw lines in terms of doctrine, of discipline and of morality. The further they go down that road the further they distance themselves from the creator and redeemer God, whose purpose is quite the opposite, to integrate and harmonise the whole of creation.

The theme of this book has been predominantly about relationships and connections and having started with young people it seems quite appropriate to finish where we began, for if we seek to find a reason why people have an active Christian faith the answer, time and time again, is because of their families, their parents and quite often their grandparents. It is often said that faith is caught, not taught, but that is too simplistic, and if what we have been saying about the way in which the Good News is passed on applies to anyone ,it applies particularly to young people. More than anything they need to be loved, to be valued and to be able to become what God has created them to be, and in addition they need to be able to make the connection between the love that they receive and the one who is the source of that love, Jesus.

Bulrushes is probably typical of church mums and babies groups all over the world. It takes place in the Church hall and for a small fee, paid each week, Mothers and carers can avail themselves of space, toys and company to alleviate the difficulties of life on your own with one or two under school age toddlers, especially when Dad is away on business for a week. There is no outwardly Christian activity, but there are always two or three church members there to talk to the young women, and to rescue the odd disaster. The Vicar makes it his business to be there for at least some of the two hours, and it is his opportunity to get to know young mothers and families in the community without the problems associated nowadays with potentially indiscrete situations. As a result the group produces a steady stream of babies for Baptism, a small proportion of whom gradually become absorbed into the Church community.

There are a few obvious opportunities to introduce mums and babies to the Church, especially at Christmas and Easter, with animals appropriate to the particular season, and mothers can enjoy being in church with their children, without the embarrassment of feeling that they are the obvious parents of the naughtiest child in the world! Occasionally, it is the child who comes to church, perhaps through a school friend, and ultimately the Mother, who at one stage approaches the Church to collect her child muttering – 'You won't get me going in there!' – finds herself, to her surprise, being Confirmed by the Bishop a few years later.

Children find churches fascinating. They are awe struck by their size, they love being able to use the acoustics to listen to their own voices. Altars, candles, pulpits, Stations of the Cross, organs, stained glass windows, crucifixes and pulpits provide endless opportunities to teach about Jesus and about the Church.

The children get drawn into the life of the Church and they see others singing in the choir, or becoming acolytes with small but important duties to perform. But they may also spend the first thirty to forty minutes of the service in Sunday school or Junior Church, where there is a great variety of activity, before going into church as the Communion itself is celebrated. They gradually learn that this is a time to be quiet and that it is a very special part of church, though of course there are occasions when they are restless enough for even the Vicar to wonder if he is flogging a dead horse. However, Mr and Mrs Dontapprove have never liked the children in church, and he is not about to give them satisfaction.

Since most churches of this style are not particularly large, there is plenty of opportunity for the different ages to get to know each other, and the benefits to all ages are clear for all to see.

And then there comes the time which the faithful parent dreads when the child, or children, say they don't want to go to church because its boring, or they don't like so-and-so, or sadly, far too often, they say – Daddy never goes to church so why should we? And there are limits to the times one can say, 'Daddy gets home very late every evening and this is his only chance of peace and quiet', and still be convincing.

And I think the answer is that lots of things that are boring are still worth doing, like maths, and tidying your room, and practising the piano; and yes, Mum and Dad get bored. But we think its important to worship God as a family and when you are older we will let you gradually make up your own mind. And the children will know just how important the parents' faith is to them. They are very astute in that way, and if the parents' stance is consistent with their lives, then the right connections will be made.

And eventually it seems the offspring doesn't come to church except possibly at Christmas or Easter. And you look back at their childhood and ask yourself what have they absorbed through the umpteen years of church nurture. Not much in the way of knowing the Bible, because sometimes it seemed as if the only thing they did was colour in doubtful pictures of Jesus and the disciples, or listen to boring stories of unlikely children who loved Jesus and wanted to be like him. No wonder they have had enough of church and will probably never go again – what is this generation coming to…?

But the answer is rather different, I believe. In spite of the inadequacies of our efforts, and the shortcomings of the Church we leave rather more than we think we do with those who have been through our hands. For what we have been doing is constructing signposts, or reference points, whose impact is quite invisible until someone or something triggers a reaction. That is why it is so important that all the senses are engaged in worship which not only involves us actively, but also in the building we use and the artefacts and the colours and the sounds which provide the accompaniment and the backdrop.

It is such a pity that there is a tendency for those involved with the young in church to assume that everything that involves normal liturgy and ceremonial in church is a turn off for the children. But hang on a minute, the kids love dressing up, and marching; and they do have a natural affinity for symbolism and ceremonial, and are fascinated by churches and their furnishings – SO LONG AS someone takes the trouble to show them and answer their questions.

But what is absolutely central to the whole exercise is that those who seek to bring young people into the Church, to discover a need to know more about God, are prepared to commit themselves not just to the work of devising and organising a program, but crucially to getting to know their charges and become their friends.

This applies right across the age range, from toddler to teenager, and most particularly, where a community has had the luxury of continuity of ministry to the young, this can be a very important factor in the smooth transition from childhood to adulthood. Sadly, everyone is so busy that it is almost impossible to find people who are prepared to give themselves consistently to this work, and the best one can hope for is to get about one in three or four days a month.

In addition, the childrens' timetables are equally congested, because parents are so concerned that their offspring should have every opportunity that is going to become star: swimmers, rugby players, horse riders, linguists, dancers, musicians, tennis players, and so on.

Here is just one way in which we tackled the problem in a school which worked a six day week. We ran a "Quest" group for children 12 to 13 onwards. Because of the time pressure, we used about three Saturdays each term. They arrived at 4 o'clock after games and other activities and we started off with games which were designed to get the young people to be at ease in each other's company and to let their hair down a bit. We took the opportunity to make some sort of reference to Biblical or Christian topics, so a game that involved the guidance of blindfolded victims across stepping stones in a river inevitably meant that the Jordan featured, or was it the Red Sea? Then followed a simple supper – in the early days it was for about ten, or so, of roughly the same year group – and then afterwards we had a serious look at some aspect of Jesus of Nazareth. On one occasion we put together a huge puzzle, each piece of which had a bible reference of something of

Jesus' life and ministry and we all pieced it together to reveal the whole Jesus – on another occasion we might play part of a video – Zeffirelli's Jesus of Nazareth was very effective, and, as in every session, we let the youngsters set their own agenda as to which way the discussion went. We finished off by going to the school chapel and having a simple service, to which we invited those who had come to fetch them and the whole thing finished at eight o'clock.

After these had been going for some time a small number of the children came and said they really would like more time to discuss the topics which we had only touched on – particularly because the Saturday evenings had a few whose interest span was limited. So we invited them to come in the lunch hour for a Bible Study each week and persuaded the school kitchens to lay on a ploughman's lunch for them. These became regular features even though the numbers were small.

Our experience of these times convinced us that, where opportunities were scarce, it was better to have a few well-planned sessions of about four hours' length, rather than to attempt shorter weekly meetings where lateness could upset the whole session.

Having a meal as the focus of the proceedings was the natural thing to do, well before the advent of Alpha courses and, of course, well established in Jewish and first century Christian circles!

We took no credit for the fact that several of the group were confirmed after two years, something that we had advertised from the beginning. Apart from that, we don't know in any real sense how these young people developed spiritually, but we still hear from a few to a greater or lesser degree and we trust that as we read in the Bible – "My word will not return void." – and as Jesus himself said – "If I am lifted up I will draw all men to me".

We hear these days a great deal about 'Youth culture' and the seeming detachment from what the rest of us would call ordinary life. Much of this is the creation of a section of the commercial world which has latched on to the opportunities presented by the spending power of the young. While we concede that it has its icons and its fashions, there is no longer the ideological conflict that their parents' generation experienced. When the externals are peeled away we find underneath the same insecure, opinionated, muddled, energetic, emotional, altruistic, young adult that we were ourselves; and we know that they often won't listen to us or take advice from us, and they won't notice what we do for them or how we suffer with them. But eventually they will concede, if only to themselves, that they are glad we were around, and glad that they were inveigled, or coerced into seeing this or learning that.

But one thing is clear. The urge to know whether a young person is converted or committed, the temptation to spell out the precise route of the spiritual journey is something which we must resist. Particularly in the teen years young people are so unsure of where they stand in so many different aspects of their development that this is a time in which we simply have to watch on the sidelines, but remain consistently available to them, even when they appear to have rejected everything that once appeared to attract them. The practice of encouraging young people to make a once for all commitment is so easily misconceived that there is more danger of damage than of growth. When God speaks to anyone and they hear, they will make their own decision in their own time.

(If the matter is manipulated or pushed in anyway, any resulting commitment may not be to the god whom we know in Jesus, but the god whom we carefully monitor and proscribe and keep down to the size we can manage.)

And then, after many years, they will find the person they

want to marry, and they will come to church to be married, and then when they look at the bundle which they have created, they will know that only the Church can say what in their hearts they know is the right way for this new life and its new journey.

Chapter 12

THE VISIBLE AND INVISIBLE CHURCH

Now the whole world had one language and a common speech. As men moved eastward they found a plain in Shinar and settled there. They said to each other, 'Come, let's make bricks and bake them thoroughly.' They used brick instead of stone, and tar for mortar. Then they said, 'Come, let us build ourselves a city with a tower that reaches to the heavens, so that we may make a name for ourselves and not be scattered over the face of the whole earth.' But the Lord came down to see the city and the tower that the men were building. The Lord said, 'If as one people speaking the same language they have begun to do this, then nothing they plan to do will be impossible for them. Come, let us go down and confuse their language so they will not understand each other.' So the Lord scattered them from there over all the earth, and they stopped building the city. That is why it was called Babel – because there the Lord confused the language of the whole world. From there the Lord scattered them over the face of the whole earth.

Let us suppose – as I have already suggested – that the early chapters of Genesis are not (as they appear to be) a retrospective account of the universe's early history but actually an aspiration of how a perfect world might be, and how that world was (or perhaps is) compromised by the paradox of

God's Creation the human being. Let us make a name for ourselves – and thereby draw a line around us which we can use to our advantage (and the rest of the world's disadvantage). Let us decide to exclude the undesirables from our club – we only accept university graduates, people with the right skills, communicants of the Church of England, those who speak proper, members of the European Union, the Commonwealth, the Tory (or Labour) Party, and so on.

Of course we all speak different languages when we define our separate identities. Anyone who walked into a cricket club, an orchestral rehearsal or a clergy meeting would experience that. Where there are more comprehensive boundaries the language differences reflect this as they do culturally, politically and economically. Yet with the technological and communication revolution the trend is clearly the other way, and that results in tensions in all areas. It is not that this is a new phenomenon but that the trend towards globalization also heightens the feelings of insecurity to a greater degree. So the desire for our own identity runs contrary to the benefits of free trade, open frontiers and a common language.

The beginning of the Second World War saw our family in an 18th-century brick house which had originally been an inn in the little hamlet where we lived close to the salt marshes of the river Dee, next door to the Mersey. We were part of a cluster of fairly substantial houses with a couple of cottages and a large manor house, which was concealed by the trees in its grounds. Our two immediate neighbours were a couple who had a nursery garden and a family who were members of one of the shipping families of the Mersey. Immediately opposite our house was a dilapidated farmhouse which had been empty since we had moved there in 1937 and which was surrounded by overgrown trees and a garden that had run wild. One balmy summer evening in 1940 at the height of the

Blitz a large furniture van came down our road and proceeded to empty its meagre contents into the derelict house. Mother, Father and five children appeared and gradually they settled in to what must have been a very spartan existence (and their capacity to improve it was obviously limited). For Father was a docker in Wallasey and Mother had been a ladies' maid and they had lost all their possessions when their house was bombed. Not long after they came their fourth child died of jaundice but the three remaining younger children gradually became close friends and along with our other young neighbours we became a gang which invented all sorts of games and fantasies which the freedom of those days made possible. We made dens, navigated the rafts on the pond and climbed the trees to our hearts' content, with little interference from grownups.

These memories have become very symbolic to me, for they speak of the possibility of a community where social and economic barriers do not and need not exist and people of very varying gifts and assets can develop mutual understanding and appreciation. Of course as we grew up we went our separate ways educationally, vocationally and geographically. But the idea of a community which is a mixture with representatives from all walks of life is much more than a sentimental aspiration; it is a vision expressed in Isaiah and in the Gospel of Jesus.

If, however, we look at the way the world is developing we will see the exact opposite of the above. The present constraints of accessibility in employment and in commercial life mean that more and more we are dividing ourselves into discrete economic and social divisions at every scale one can think of. In its worst expression we can think of the favellas (squatter settlements) of Sao Paolo and the security gates and guards which protect the super-rich in the same city. The leafier parts of the commuter belt round London are so sought after that nurses, teachers and the less skilled either have to live miles away or they live in a council estate which presents such a contrast with the rest of the settlement that it takes on an almost ghetto-like status.

But this is nothing when compared to the global level. The countries of the temperate west have built on their climatic and biotic advantages to establish an incredibly wealthy life-style, much of it stemming from the exploitation of natural resources in less developed areas. The latter, on the other hand, have been at the mercy of nations which are economically superior to them and have therefore always maintained their stranglehold on those with whom they now trade (rather than plunder). The high incidence of sickness, of famine and of land degradation – all interrelated – in the developing world have been significantly influenced by the introduction of farming methods and medicine imported from the west. And the stranglehold that the west has exerted over the financial situation of endemic national debt inevitably means that the gap between rich and poor is getting bigger.

But that is the nature of the beast – capitalism. Since the dismantling of the communist systems it has spread throughout the world – with the notable exception of Cuba and maybe one or two others. There has been nothing to challenge the notion which pervades every area of life – that life is about competition; that what matters is climbing the league table and displacing those above you. Once there, all energies have to be directed to maintaining the position and resisting the efforts of everyone else to dislodge you. This pervades international, national, regional and local life – not only in matters economic but also in education, in sport, and almost every other facet of our lives.

In addition (but probably part of the same) there are the

constraints of accessibility and of economies of scale, which further cause differentiation at every scale. In this country shops in the smaller settlements are put out of business as huge supermarkets mushroom on the edge of towns. A farming estate village with attractive houses is patronized by the wealthier house-hunters who, with two cars, can ensure that they can access supplies from the supermarket and other facilities on the nearby edge-of-town industrial estates. The village shop closes, as does the school, which is too small to be viable. The advent of off-licences and drinking at home saw that the pub closed some time ago. All these redundant buildings have become private homes and the resulting settlement is a monochrome detached housing estate serving a narrow sector of the socio-economic spectrum with no communal activities at all, since they all have cars and n channels of television.

On a much more general level the whole economic and social revolution has dismantled the traditional structure of society – again. For we have to remember that history will show a succession of changes which have to be taken on board and understood if the right sort of adjustments are to be made. But the worldwide communications revolution from the steam train to the aeroplane to the radio and television to computers and the internet means that the whole idea of community is threatened as children move away from parents, as businessmen are forced to relocate every few years, and as the traditional foci of community life give way to the national and international topics of interest.

And the Church has been struggling to keep up with all this and, tied as it is constitutionally, it has been particularly difficult for the Church of England. Both in the old established towns and in the country the Church of England has had expectations put on it which it hasn't got the resources to provide. As the national Church it has been expected to provide baptisms and funerals and to a lesser extent marriages as well as a regular Sunday service, and also to be a focus for national celebrations and crises. At the same time there has been a drift away from regular attendance and financial support as religious and scientific developments have affected belief and social practice.

The non-established churches have fared little better. The Nonconformist churches – which broke away from the established Church largely on grounds of theology and doctrine – have had the ground taken from under them by the increasingly inclusive nature of Anglicanism. The Catholic Church suffers through its centralization and tradition and its consequent inability to attract new priests and lay members.

There are pockets which buck the trend. Mostly these are evangelical churches which serve a fairly narrow constituency and whose style depends on whether they are serving inner-city or suburban communities (where there is a large catchment area). They are divided between C of E, Nonconformist and new House Churches which are autonomous and very tightly-knit associations. But they all share the same limitations of being too oriented towards personal salvation and domestic morality and being uninterested in wider and global issues, apart from the desire to extend their own visible boundaries.

And I say visible, for there are countless people who have reacted against what purported to be Christian in some institution of other but which was blatantly unchristian in character. We all can think of examples, such as the school chaplain who told a class of thirteen-year-olds that unless they were Christian they would go to hell; the assistant chaplain who compromised a female colleague while he was engaged to a young woman who lived abroad; the numerous occurrences of sexual abuse by priests and many of the historical records which are recorded from past centuries; the importation to a parish of a healing team consisting of healers and subjects from a nearby charismatic church to speak about and demonstrate the power of healing. None of these invalidate the Gospel of Jesus but they close the gateway to conscious faith and Church commitment for those who have too little acquaintance with the wider Church to counter its aberrations.

Perhaps one of the commonest attitudes in modern times is the number of people who say that they admire Jesus and do their best to follow or imitate him, but they have a problem with the Church for the reasons stated above and – yes – partly as an excuse. But it is true to say that many of these are shining examples of what Jesus meant in the parable of the Sheep and the Goats in the second half of Matthew's 25th chapter, also quoted in a previous chapter:

> *'Then the righteous will answer him, "Lord, when did we see you hungry and feed you, or thirsty and give you something to drink? When did we see you a stranger and invite you in, or needing clothes and clothe you? When did we see you sick or in prison and go to visit you?" The King will reply, "I tell you the truth, whatever you did for one of the least of these brothers of mine, you did for me".'*

The more prescriptive a church is the harder it is for thoughtful people to identify with it, and the more blurred the boundaries are between faith and lack of faith on this earth the more true it is to the Gospel of Jesus.

The problem with the visible Church is that it is being stifled by its professionalism. It has a huge administrative machinery which employs large numbers of staff. With a shortage of good clergy and rationalization of parish oversight it is still creating more and more posts for so-called experts in education, counselling, industry, ecumenism, communications and a host of others. Parishes are increasingly told that they only qualify for a half-time ministry (they are the lucky ones) or that their benefice is getting another two parishes, bringing the total number to seven.

But the one thing that is needed is pastoral oversight for those isolated in parish ministry. They don't need a gaggle of experts to tell them what to do: what they do need is support and developing a relationship with their bishop, who at the moment spends most of his time in committees and in high-level interactions with various regional and national bodies when what is needed is low-level interaction (especially with those who are exercising a priestly ministry).

The other problem with the visible church is that it is too hooked on religion. An active church is one which can demonstrate a full programme of meetings and services throughout the week... so there are Bible study groups, prayer groups, various groups for different sections of the congregations, committee meetings and so on. It's not so much that these exist, it is more the fact that they are seen as being proof of the effectiveness of the church: that there is salvation in the increase of church activity.

None of these things, however, are matters of critical importance unless the visible church excludes the rest. The more the Church draws lines around the tangible expression of Christian faith the more damage is done to the Church of God. And one of the ways this happens is the exclusiveness of the Church. It is absolutely right that one has to qualify to be able to teach and to preach and to celebrate and administer the sacraments. Perhaps one of the greatest dangers comes from the Christian activist whose only qualification is his zeal. But when it comes to who may receive Christ it is another matter: the idea that you have to understand theology is thankfully receding, and the Anglican move to admit children to Communion before confirmation a great step forward. Yet I can't help feeling that if we don't invite everyone to share around Christ's supper table, whatever their status, then we are compromising the very heart of what the Gospel is all about. I think it would be very unlikely that anyone would abuse that invitation any more than we do ourselves by the carelessness with which we receive God in our frantic rush to get the service over so that we can rush around being Christian.

But back to the visible and the invisible church. The situation can be compared to an iceberg. The visible part of the iceberg is only a small fraction of the whole mass. If part of this is removed it simply means that more of the invisible submerged part is revealed, but if tons of already visible ice is added so more of the iceberg is submerged to a deeper level.

So I would echo the observations and instructions of Ortiz and say, 'Come to Mass on Sunday. Enter into the whole liturgy – the confession and absolution – open your mind to the ministry of the word and its relevance to us today. Join in with the creed,' possibly adding, 'Lord, help my unbelief, and enter into the prayers as they take you out into the community and the world. With the elements of bread and wine offer yourself to God – and know that in the sharing of the bread and the wine Christ becomes present in your very being – and God gives you his living breath to be his creative love in the community, one which becomes wider than you could imagine.'

And then I would say, 'and I don't want to see you again until next Sunday.'